*shop 'til
you drop*

shop 'til you drop

Consumer Behavior and American Culture

Arthur Asa Berger

Illustrations by the Author

ROWMAN & LITTLEFIELD PUBLISHERS, INC.
Lanham • Boulder • New York • Toronto • Oxford

ROWMAN & LITTLEFIELD PUBLISHERS, INC.

Published in the United States of America
by Rowman & Littlefield Publishers, Inc.
A wholly owned subsidiary of The Rowman & Littlefield Publishing Group, Inc.
4501 Forbes Boulevard, Suite 200, Lanham, MD 20706
www.rowmanlittlefield.com

P.O. Box 317, Oxford OX2 9RU, UK

British Library Cataloguing in Publication Information Available

Library of Congress Cataloging-in-Publication Data

Berger, Arthur Asa, 1933–
Shop 'til you drop : consumer behavior and American culture / Arthur Asa Berger.
    p. cm.
Includes bibliographical references and index.
ISBN 0-7425-3690-4 (cloth : alk. paper) — ISBN 0-7425-3691-2 (pbk. : alk. paper)
 1. Consumer behavior—United States. 2. Consumer behavior—Social aspects—
United States. 3. Consumers' preferences—Psychological aspects—United States.
I. Title.

HF5415.33.U6B47 2005
658.8'342—dc22

                                                          2005011765

Printed in the United States of America

∞™ The paper used in this publication meets the minimum requirements of
American National Standard for Information Sciences—Permanence of Paper
for Printed Library Materials, ANSI/NISO Z39.48-1992.

In memory of Marguerite Young

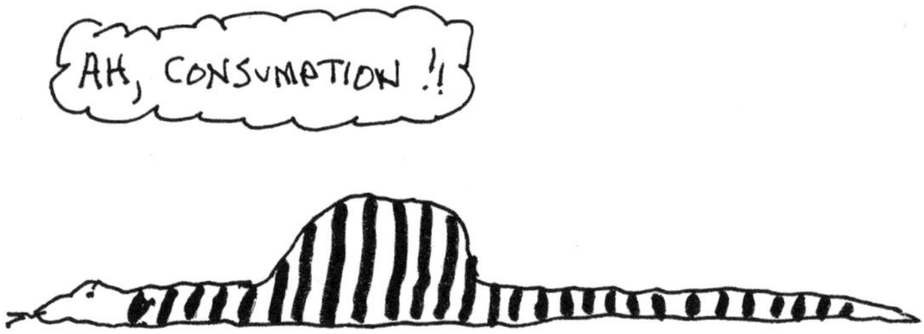
AH, CONSUMPTION !!

CONTENTS

Preface   ix

Acknowledgments   xiii

1 What Are Consumer Cultures?   1

2 Profiles in Consumption   21

3 The Act of Consumption   45

4 Perspectives on Consumption   69

5 The Semiotics of Shopping   89

6 Malls and the American Consumer Culture   99

7 Tourism and Consumer Culture   111

8 Buyer's Remorse   119

References   127

Index   129

About the Author   135

As a society, we are embedded in a culture of consumption. Neil Postman . . . notes that by the age of forty the average American will have seen well over one million commercials and have "close to another million to go before his first social security check." In order to comprehend the impact of all this advertising on society we must learn how to see through advertisements, for they are not just messages about goods and services but social and cultural texts about ourselves. (Frith 1997, 1)

—**Katherine T. Frith,** *Undressing the Ad:*
Reading Culture in Advertising

Consumers appeared to have experienced shopping fatigue in September and October after heroic spending in the summer, when tax rebates fueled a surge in sales. The latest figures suggest that consumers are now regaining their energy. (*Financial Times,* December 12, 2003, p. 2)

—**Christopher Swann and Neil Buckley, "Economic Reports"**

PREFACE

This book deals with the American passion for consuming, with the fact that on many—I would say too many—occasions we shop 'til we drop. The term *passion* here suggests a powerful emotional surge that, so to speak, "consumes" or dominates a person. Think, for example, of that all-consuming passion—romantic love. Statistics on divorce in the United States suggest that many people who metaphorically "consume" one another in marriage sooner or later experience "buyer's regret." In the best tradition of American consuming, they "return" their partners (via divorce). Then they generally shop around some more (what we call dating) and move on to other marriages, which is why marriage in America can be described as serial monogamy.

The second meaning of *passion* involves consuming things, such as objects and services, with emotional excitement and fervor. That is the topic I am most concerned with, though it is not unrelated to the first meaning of the word. The term *consumer culture* has become commonplace in recent years. Most people now live in what sociologists, economists, culture critics, and other kinds of scholars tell us are consumer cultures. But what, exactly, is a consumer culture, and how do these consumer cultures affect our lives?

As a first step in understanding what consumer cultures are, let me say
something about the nature of language and how we make sense of words.
Swiss linguist Ferdinand de Saussure explained in his book *A Course in
General Linguistics* that "concepts are purely differential and defined not
by their positive content but negatively by their relations with the other
terms of the system" (Saussure 1966, 117). So we learn what a word means,
Saussure argues, by finding out what it doesn't mean.

It is the relation of a term to other terms in a system of words and concepts that determines meaning, not content per se. Or, as Saussure put it,
the most precise characteristic of a concept "is in being what the others
are not." He adds, "In languages there are only differences. . . . The entire mechanism of language . . . is based on oppositions" (Saussure 1966,
120–21).

So, in order to understand what a consumer culture is, we have to see
what its opposite might be—which would be something like a *production*
culture, or a sustenance culture, or a scarcity culture. We have to use a concept that is oppositional but not a negation, such as a "nonconsumer culture." This is because relations determine meaning, and the basic relationship is one of opposition (that is, another opposing concept) rather than
negation. We make sense of the world by seeing things in relation to oppositions: rich and poor, happy and sad, large and small, and so on. But what
is the best polar opposite of a consumer culture—or, to be more explicit, a
consumption-dominated culture? I'll say more about this matter later, in
chapter 1 of the text.

In researching this book, I checked on books dealing with consumer
cultures at Amazon.com (itself one of the more interesting innovations in
selling and consumption) and found thousands of titles listed there. The
search engine Google lists hundreds of thousands of websites dealing, in
one way or another, with consumer cultures. Why is there so much interest in this subject? Because, I would suggest, all the people who write
these books and set up their websites believe that the consumer cultures
in which we find ourselves play an important role in our lives, in our families, and in all the institutions of society, such as religion, politics, and
the arts.

If these writers (and others interested in the subject) are correct, when
we go shopping, when we go on dates, when we choose our mates, when
we attend a religious service, when we choose which college to attend,
when we go to the movies, when we buy a pair of jeans—one could go on
endlessly—we are playing our role in the development of our consumer

cultures. There are continual calculations of gains and losses, expenses and benefits that we make all the time. What roles are these consumer cultures playing in our lives, and how is the fact that you are a consumer—that is, a shopper—affecting your life? The answer, you will find, is interesting, important, and perhaps—in some ways—surprising.

ACKNOWLEDGMENTS

I am grateful to my editor, Brenda Hadenfeldt, for her encouragement and for her help with this book. Since I had the good fortune to meet her at an International Communication Association meeting in San Francisco a number of years ago, we have had a very fine and productive relationship. Not every editor has the courage she demonstrated when she published my academic mystery, *The Mass Comm Murders,* in which five media theorists murder one another—but only after explaining their theories of media.

I also want to thank Brenda's colleagues at Rowman & Littlefield for their contributions to this book: my production editor, Kärstin Painter; my copyeditor, Christianne Thillen; the cover designer, Piper Furbush; and everyone else involved with its production.

I have, in a few places in this book, drawn on discussions from other works of mine—namely, *Ads, Fads, and Consumer Culture* and *Deconstructing Travel*—but these sections represent a very small percentage of the material used for this book. The text also includes "Consumer Culture Factoids" taken from here and there. In some cases, I have slightly modified the language or the arrangements of elements in the factoids, but never the meaning. To add a bit of color to my analyses, I offer various boxed inserts of material relevant to the topics being discussed.

ARE YOU WASTING MONEY?

If you are shopping each week for what you will eat that week—"Meal Planning"—YOU ARE WASTING MONEY!

That's what the grocery stores want you to do. You may get a few bargains, but you are forced to buy things that are high priced because you NEED them.

WHAT IF YOU HAD YOUR OWN STORE AT HOME? Yes, that's the concept of STOCKPILING.

HOW CAN I AFFORD TO STOCKPILE?

TERI'S SHOPPING LIST is designed each week to stock your shelves the cheapest way possible. After you stick with me for a few weeks, you will begin to see how much you have and how little you spend, with very little effort on your part (I do the laborious part).

—**www.thegrocerygame.com/index.dfm?goto=con_more_info**
(accessed December 28, 2003)

1

WHAT ARE CONSUMER CULTURES?

What exactly are consumer cultures? How do we define the term? And if the concept of "consumer culture" means anything, there must be some other kind of culture opposing it, as Saussure (1966) has suggested in his analysis of language. In this chapter I define consumer cultures, locate the origin of contemporary consumer cultures in religious thought, discuss the theory that there are not one but four different consumer cultures, and relate consumer cultures to the development of postmodernism.

DEFINING CONSUMER CULTURES

Consumer cultures are cultures in which the personal consumption of goods and services becomes an all-powerful force. This force dominates other matters, such as the need for investment in the public sector to take care of the education, housing, health, and other needs of the general public. In these cultures, advertising and marketing play all-important roles, and privatism—a focus on one's personal interests and desires, in contrast to a sense of public responsibility for others and for one's society—tends to dominate most people's thinking and behavior.

All cultures are based on consumption. That's because people need to eat, need to clothe themselves, need to have some kind of housing, need to have ways of teaching the young, and need to have access to medical attention.

There are, of course, still some scattered traditional cultures (we used to call them primitive) that are subsistence ones—in which individuals produce the food that they need and take care of other needs with little need for purchasing goods and services from others. But most of these subsistence cultures, or, more precisely, the tribes that live that way, are rapidly being transformed. More and more, they too are becoming consumer cultures.

If people are to produce goods and services, there must be others who will consume them; so production and consumption are, if you think about it, two sides of the same coin. In consumer societies, as critics of consumer cultures argue, the forces of personal or private consumption are out of control. They are like a cancer that cannot stop growing, relegating other forces in society to a secondary status, if not ignoring most of them. So it is a question of degree. Where does a normal amount of consumption "end" and an obsessive concern with consumption and overconsumption begin?

Mike Featherstone, a British sociologist, suggests there are three basic perspectives on consumer cultures. He writes, in his book *Consumer Culture and Postmodernism*:

> First is the view that consumer culture is premised upon the expansion of capitalist commodity production which has given rise to a vast accumulation of material culture in the form of consumer goods and sites for purchase and consumption. This has resulted in the growing salience of leisure and consumption activities in contemporary Western societies which, although greeted as leading to a greater egalitarianism and individual freedom by some, is regarded by others as increasing the capacity for ideological manipulation and "seductive" containment of the population from some alternative set of "better" social relations. Second, there is the more strictly sociological view that the satisfaction derived from goods relates to their socially structured access in a zero sum game in which satisfaction and status depend upon displaying and sustaining differences within conditions of inflation. The focus here is upon the different ways in which people use goods in order to create social bonds or distinctions. Third, there is the question of the emotional pleasures of consumption, the dreams and desires which become celebrated in consumer cultural imagery and particular sites of consumption, which variously generate direct bodily excitement and aesthetic pleasure. (Featherstone 1991, 13)

I will be exploring a number of these topics in this book, which focuses a considerable amount of attention on the social and cultural aspects of consumption. When we purchase something it is, generally speaking, an individual act; but it is connected to any number of things relating to our sociocultural identity. The act of consumption, in fact, is just the tip of the consumer culture iceberg.

CONSUMING PASSIONS

We must remember that consuming is an *activity*—a person decides, for one reason or another, to buy something. It can either be an object, such as a car or a house or this book, or a service, such as attending a college or university or taking a trip to some exotic place or seeing a doctor. The two words in this section's heading are quite interesting. *Consuming*, according to various dictionaries, means a variety of things, such as "to do away with and destroy" (as in a fire), "to squander and spend in a wasteful manner," and "to utilize economic goods and services."

The term *passion* comes from the Latin word *pati*, which means "to suffer," "to have intense, overpowering emotions or feelings," and "to feel ardent affection and love to some object of deep interest and desire." People sometimes use the phrase "all-consuming passion" to describe a person who is overcome by certain feelings and cannot act reasonably and rationally. Often the phrase relates to romantic love, but it has broader applications. It is

All cultures are based on consumption to some degree. Where does a normal amount of consumption end and obsessive overconsumption begin?

CONSUMER CULTURE FACTOID

Most American homes have two color television sets, central air conditioning, a dishwasher, a microwave oven, a VCR or DVD player, a personal computer, a cell phone, a cordless phone, and an answering machine.

The American Marketplace: Demographics and Spending Patterns, 6th ed., by the New Strategist editors (Ithaca, NY: New Strategist Publications, 2003), 7.

what Featherstone (1991) alluded to when he discussed the "pleasure" people get from buying things.

My wife, interestingly enough, often talks about having to "fall in love with a pair of shoes" before she'll buy them. I, on the other hand, tend to leave love and passion out of the equation (at least I've convinced myself that such is the case) when I purchase things—relying on advice from *Consumer Reports* when possible, on the price of the object in which I'm interested, or the fact that it will "do the job." We are two different consumer personalities, a subject I will discuss in more detail in my analysis of the psychological aspects of consumption.

The passion I am most concerned with in this book is the passion for consuming, which we find, for example, in shopaholics who "shop 'til they drop." There are, also, compulsive shoppers who cannot restrain themselves from buying things—shoes that don't fit them, things they don't need—because of the various gratifications they get from the act of buying things. These people are ill and need psychological help to deal with their affliction. But where do we draw the line between compulsive shoppers and ordinary people, who, it turns out, spend a great deal of their leisure time shopping?

THE SACRED ROOTS OF CONSUMER CULTURE

Contemporary sociologists, economists, and culture critics are not the first thinkers to be concerned with consumer culture and with philosophical and other problems related to consumption. Theologians and others, over the millennia, have had theories about topics such as how to live, how to think about work, and what to do with money. In the Middle Ages, there was a great interest in asceticism and minimizing one's work and one's consumption. But not everyone accepted the belief that the ascetic lifestyle, generally associated with Catholicism, was the best one.

John Calvin (1509–1564), an influential Protestant theologian, speculated about these matters and attacked asceticism. As quoted in *European Origins of American Thought,* Calvin wrote:

> If we are only to pass through the earth, we ought undoubtedly to make such a use of its blessings as will rather assist rather than retard us in our journey. It is not without reason, therefore, that Paul advises us to use the world as though we used it not, and to buy with the same disposition with which we sell (I Cor. Vii:30,31). But as this is a difficult subject, and there is danger of falling into one of two opposite errors, let us endeavor to proceed on safe ground, that we may avoid both extremes. (Van Tassel and McAharen 1969, 11–12)

The extremes Calvin cautioned against were extravagant excesses and intemperance, on one side, and life-denying austerity and asceticism on the other.

IF WE ARE ONLY TO PASS THROUGH THE EARTH, WE OUGHT TO MAKE USE OF ITS BLESSINGS...

Calvin continues his explanation:

> It must be laid down as a principle, that the use of the gifts of God is not er-
> roneous when it is directed to the same end for which the Creator himself has
> created and appointed them for us; since he has created them for our benefit,
> not for our injury. . . . Now, if we consider to what end he has created the var-
> ious kinds of aliments, we shall find that he intended to provide not only for
> our necessity, but likewise for our pleasure and delight. So in clothing, he has
> had in view not mere necessity, but propriety and decency. In herbs, trees, and
> fruits, besides their various uses, his design has been to gratify us by graceful
> forms and pleasant odours. (Van Tassel and McAharen 1969, 12–13)

Calvin argues, then, that people should discard the ascetic perspective on
life, an inhuman philosophy that "malignantly deprives us of the lawful enjoyment of the Divine beneficence, but which cannot be embraced 'til it has
despoiled man of all his senses, and reduced him to a senseless block" (Van
Tassel and McAharen 1969, 13). We have to draw a line, Calvin argues, between the ascetic extreme, which focuses on abstinence and reducing life to
its bare necessities, and the opposite extreme, which involves intemperance
in eating and drinking and "fastidiousness in our furniture, our habitations,
and our apparel," as well as other kinds of behavior that distract people
from their need to look after their souls.

According to Max Weber, one of the greatest sociological theorists of the
twentieth century, Calvinism and what Weber described as "the Protestant
ethic" is behind the development of capitalism. Weber's book *The Protestant
Ethic and the Spirit of Capitalism* deals with the impact of the Protestant
ethic on modern societies and its role in the development of capitalism.
What the Protestant ethic did, in essence, was loosen the grip on people's
minds of medieval notions about the value of poverty and justify consumption as something that God wants people to do, that has a divine significance.

To be able to consume, however, people need money—which means that
hard work had to be glorified, and wasting time on unprofitable pursuits
had to be attacked. Weber uses the term *asceticism* to describe the Protestant perspective on life; but it is a different kind of asceticism from the medieval, self-denying asceticism that Calvin disparaged. The Protestant ethic
did two things: it provided a diligent, hard-working workforce, and it explained to people that their place in the scheme of things was settled by
God. As Weber explained:

> The power of religious asceticism provided him [the bourgeois business-
> man] . . . with sober, conscientious, and unusually industrious workmen, who

clung to their work as to a life purpose willed by God. Finally, it gave him the comforting assurance that the unequal distribution of the goods of this world was a special dispensation of Divine Providence, which in these differences, as in particular grace, pursued secret ends unknown to men. (Weber 1958, 177)

This notion that there is a "Divine Providence" that explains the unequal distribution of wealth is a great comfort to those at the top of the pyramid, for it justifies their position there. By implication, it also suggests that efforts to ameliorate the lives of the poor are fruitless, for such efforts are against Divine Providence. At the conclusion of his book, Weber discusses the ideas of Richard Baxter, a Puritan minister, who believed that "the care for external goods should only lie on the shoulders of the 'saint like a light cloak, which can be thrown aside at any moment.' But fate decreed that the cloak should become an iron cage" (Weber 1958, 181).

Weber continues with a discussion of the changes that have taken place over the years. The spirit of this asceticism, he argues, has escaped from the cage, and "material goods have gained an increasing and finally an inexorable power over the lives of men as at no previous period in history" (Weber 1958, 181). Weber's book was published in German in 1904 and 1905, so his analysis of capitalism and critique of what we now describe as consumer culture is approximately 100 years old.

Weber adds, in rather poignant language, a lament about what has happened, suggesting also that America is where the pursuit of wealth has reached its highest development:

> No one knows who will live in this cage in the future, or whether at the end of this tremendous development entirely new prophets will arise, or there will be a mechanized petrification, embellished with a sort of convulsive self-importance. For of the last state of this cultural development, it might be truly said: "Specialists without spirit, sensualists without heart; this nullity imagines that it has attained a level of civilization never before achieved" (Weber 1958, 182)

He concludes, on the last page of his book, that it is important to give religious ideas "a significance for culture and national character which they deserve" (Weber 1958, 183).

What this discussion of Calvin and Weber suggests is that there is, indeed, an important religious or sacred dimension to our consuming passions; and the same passions and fervor that animate religious belief in people are found in a desacralized—that is, secularized—form, shaping their behavior as consumers in contemporary societies. Shopping, then, if we adopt a religious perspective on things, becomes a sacred act. But consumption, rather than lying like a light cloak upon our shoulders, now has wrapped around us, covering us completely—to adopt Baxter's metaphor—and taken control of us.

Many analysts attack our consumer cultures, characterized by continual shopping, for being grossly materialistic and repugnant (for not trying to alleviate the suffering of millions of poor and disadvantaged people); but there are some scholars with different opinions on the matter. I now turn to the work of social anthropologist Mary Douglas, who defends shopping and offers us a different approach to consumer culture—one that emphasizes its social and cultural dimensions.

THE GRID-GROUP TYPOLOGY: ARE THERE FOUR CONSUMER CULTURES?

In their book, *Cultural Theory*, social scientists Michael Thompson, Richard Ellis, and Aaron Wildavsky deal with the work of Mary Douglas, a British social anthropologist, who developed a theory that we can use to understand why individuals consume products and services the way they do. Douglas's theory deals with what she describes as grid-group relationships.

Her grid-group typology is used to deal with sociological theory and political cultures; but it also, she suggests, has implications that deal with consumer cultures and the matter of taste preferences. Thompson and coauthors explain the Douglas grid-group typology as follows:

> She argues that the variability of an individual's involvement in social life can be adequately captured by two dimensions of sociality: group and grid. *Group* refers to the extent to which an individual is incorporated into bounded units. The greater the incorporation, the more individual choice is subject to group determination. *Grid* denotes the degree to which an individual's life is circumscribed by externally imposed prescriptions. The more binding and extensive the scope of the prescriptions, the less of life that is open to individual negotiation. (Thompson, Ellis, and Wildavsky 1990, 5)

The group dimension refers to the degree to which an individual's life is shaped and sustained by membership in a group; the group's boundaries and control over individuals in the group can be strong or weak. The grid

GROUP
(Strength of Boundaries)

		Weak	Strong
GRID (Rules & Prescriptions)	**Many**	Fatalists	Elitists
	Few	Individualists	Egalitarians

dimension refers to whether there are few or many rules and prescriptions individuals have to obey.

If we take the two dimensions Douglas talks about—*group membership* (weak or strong) and *grid aspects* (few rules or numerous and varied rules and prescriptions)—we find that they generate the four political cultures, ways of life, or, as we shall see later, consumer cultures: hierarchist (elitist), fatalist, egalitarian, and individualist.

Another way to represent this relationship is in the following chart, which spells out the various relationships more directly.

Group Boundaries: Strong or Weak	Grid Aspects: Kinds and Number of Prescriptions	Way of Life: Consumer Cultures
Strong	Numerous and varied	Elitist
Weak	Numerous and varied	Fatalist (Isolates)
Strong	Few or minimal	Egalitarian (Enclavists)
Weak	Few or minimal	Individualist

This grid-group typology actually generates five cultures, but only four of these are important for our purposes. (A fifth way of life, autonomy, has very few members and is essentially based on withdrawing from society; it is of little interest to us.) Thompson and coauthors describe how the grid-group typology generates the four ways of life:

> Strong group boundaries coupled with minimal prescriptions produce social relations that are egalitarian. . . . When an individual's social environment is characterized by strong group boundaries and binding prescriptions, the resulting social relations are hierarchical [elitist]. . . . Individuals who are bound by neither group incorporation nor prescribed roles inhabit

an individualistic social context. In such an environment all boundaries are provisional and subject to negotiation. . . . People who find themselves subject to binding prescriptions and are excluded from group membership exemplify the fatalistic way of life. Fatalists are controlled from without. (Thompson, Ellis, and Wildavsky. 1990, 6–7)

So there are four consumer cultures; and each of them, it turns out, is in conflict with all of the others, yet they all need one another. Hierarchists (elitists) believe in the utility of stratification, but they are imbued with a sense of responsibility toward those below them; individualists are essentially interested in themselves and want the government to do little, except to protect their freedom to compete with others; egalitarians argue that we all have the same basic needs and tend to play down differences between people; and fatalists find themselves ordered around by others and pin their hopes on chance and luck as the means of escaping from their situation.

Elitists need stratification in order to maintain their position at the top of the ladder, so they need fatalists; egalitarians fight stratification and want to raise everyone up, especially the fatalists. And individualists need a stable society, run by elitists and themselves, in order to function.

These four cultures play an important role in the lives of the members of each culture, even though most people aren't aware of their existence. That is, they are covert, latent, or hidden, for all practical purposes. Thompson and his colleagues suggest that social scientists must, of necessity, spend a great deal of energy looking for latent or hidden aspects of social phenomena. They use this insight to offer a comment on the Marxist perspective on society:

Things are never as they seem in class societies, Marx tells us, because exploitation must be disguised for the social order to be sustained. Since rulers do not like to think of themselves as exploiters, benefiting unjustly from the labor of others, and the exploited must be kept ignorant of their subjection lest they revolt, the truth must be kept from both rulers and ruled alike. (Thompson, Ellis, and Wildavsky 1990, 149)

Marx argued that mystification is essential to the capitalist economic system; on the other hand, Thompson, Ellis, and Wildavsky suggest that mystification is an all-pervasive phenomenon that informs *every* aspect of life. Social scientists, they assert, should look for mystification everywhere, and explain its existence and how it functions wherever they find it.

Marx made an important error, our authors assert, when he failed to recognize that egalitarianism functions successfully as a critique of society and social relationships only when it is out of power. If Marx had used his formidable powers to analyze egalitarian societies as well as hierarchist/elitist and fatalist ones (read here "bourgeois" and "proletarian"), he would quite likely have changed his ideas about the need for revolution.

IN DEFENSE OF SHOPPING

In an essay titled "In Defence of Shopping," Mary Douglas redefines these four political cultures as lifestyles and substitutes the term *isolates* for fatalists and *enclavists* for egalitarians (Douglas 1997). There are, she suggests, four consumer cultures or lifestyles; and it is a person's membership in one of these four consumer cultures or lifestyles—each of which is antagonistic or in conflict with the three others—that ultimately explains that person's consumer choices.

Even though people may not be able to articulate their beliefs and values and are not aware that they belong to one of the four consumer cultures, they can recognize that their values and beliefs aren't those of members of the other consumer cultures. This recognition has important implications. It means that consumption is primarily based on cultural alignments and hostilities rather than being based on individual wants or desires.

Douglas relates consumption to these four political cultures as follows:

None of these four lifestyles (individualist, hierarchical, enclavist [egalitarian], isolated [fatalist]) is new to students of consumer behavior. What may be new and unacceptable is the point that these are the only four distinctive lifestyles to be taken into account, and the other point, that each is set up in competition with the others. Mutual hostility is the force that accounts for their stability. These four distinct lifestyles persist because they rest on incompatible organizational principles. Each culture is a way of organizing; each is predatory on the others for time and space and resources. It is hard for them to co-exist peacefully, and yet they must, for the survival of each is the guarantee of the survival of the others. Hostility keeps them going. (Douglas 1997, 19)

Douglas's grid-group theory attacks theories of consumption based on individualist psychology. She argues that when it comes to consumption, to buying things, *"cultural alignment is the strongest predictor of preferences in a wide variety of fields"* (Douglas 1997, 23; emphasis added). There is, then, if Douglas is correct, a rational basis to consumer preferences. In addition, Douglas argues, it is consumers who ultimately determine what will be sold. Though people who belong to different consumer cultures may have similar incomes (except for the fatalists/isolates, members of what we would call the "underclass," who are generally at the bottom of the income ladder), what individuals purchase and their general patterns of consumption are shaped by their membership in one of the four consumer cultures.

Douglas concludes, then, that shopping is not the expression of individual wants. The notion that it is doesn't take into account the matter of cultural bias. As she writes in the conclusion to her essay:

> The idea of consumer sovereignty in economic theory will be honoured in market research because it will be abundantly clear that the shopper sets the trends, and that new technology and new prices are adjuncts to achieving the shopper's goal. The shopper is not expecting to develop a personal identity by choice of commodities; that would be too difficult. *Shopping is agonistic, a struggle to define not what one is but what one is not.* When we include not one cultural bias, but four, and when we allow that each is bringing critiques against the others, and when we see that the shopper is adopting postures of cultural defiance, then it all makes sense. (Douglas 1997, 30; emphasis added)

The author's statement that shopping is agonistic and represents an attempt to define what one is not calls to mind Ferdinand de Saussure's linguistic theories—in particular, his statement that "concepts are purely differential and defined not by their positive content but negatively, by their relations with the other terms of the system" (Saussure 1966, 117). Let me modify what Saussure said by suggesting that "the most precise characteristic" of concepts and of lifestyles "is in being what the others are not." As the makers of 7-Up argued in their commercials a few years ago, their drink is an "un-cola."

Thompson, Ellis, and Wildavsky consider an interesting question related to this matter of preferences, which is: Are people free? They write:

Placing people in categories seems to many observers to do violence to the individual. For, they ask, if ways of life act as programs telling people what to prefer and how to behave, aren't individuals little better than automatons, robots, ciphers, mere windup toys moved by unseen hands? Solving the problem of preference formation seems to come at the expense of individual choice.

Plural ways of life, we respond, give individuals a chance for extensive, if finite choice. The existence of competing ways of organizing gives individuals knowledge of other possibilities, and the opportunity to observe how people who live according to these other ways are doing. (Thompson, Ellis, and Wildavsky 1990, 13)

What complicates this grid-group typology is that people (except for fatalists) can move from one lifestyle or consumer culture to another. Sometimes they are forced to do so—for example, when individualists who are making a very high salary are fired because their company is purchased by another company; or when they are injured and unable to work. They may end up, then, in the egalitarian camp—or even in the fatalist one.

Thompson and his colleagues argue that there are "organizational imperatives created by the interaction of the grid and group dimensions that compel people to behave in ways that maintain their way of life" (Thompson, Ellis, and Wildavsky 1990, 262). This is because we are social animals, and our behavior is profoundly affected by (though not always strictly determined by) the consumer culture to which we belong and the rules and prescriptions of that consumer culture.

Many different reasons can be given to explain a person's consumption preferences—for consumer products and services or for politicians—but they all stem from two fundamental factors: first, the groups to which people belong and, second, the number and kinds of rules and prescriptions to which they adhere.

Some questions are not answered by the grid-group typology. How do we explain the consumption behavior of children? How do ethnic groupings, religious groupings, and racial groupings relate to the grid-group typology? According to Douglas's grid-group theory, these matters are secondary to grid-group relationships; and that may in fact be the case. Douglas argues that one's consumer culture and lifestyle are more important than one's ethnicity or other demographic factors. That may explain why some marketers focus on ZIP codes or magazine purchases, which presumably link people according to their lifestyles and consumer cultures rather than their ethnicity, race, and religion. It may also be that within various racial, ethnic, gender, and other groups there are the four consumer cultures at work, so that the idea of consumer cultures explains consumer behavior in all the demographic categories.

CONSUMER CULTURES AND OTHER KINDS OF CULTURES

I have argued that if the concept "consumer culture" is to have any meaning, there must, as Saussure would explain, be some other kind of culture that exists in opposition to it. I suggested that what might be called "subsistence culture" plays this role. I am thinking here of relatively primitive, preliterate, isolated agricultural communities. Consumer cultures are characterized by continual consumption, far beyond what is necessary for people to survive. Subsistence cultures, on the other hand, are characterized by minimal consumption—consumption of goods and services by others does not play an important role in daily life.

These two kinds of cultures represent opposite extremes, what Max Weber would call "ideal types." In between are cultures with varying degrees of consumption and consuming passions or subsistence living. In consumer cultures, the focus is on things desired but not absolutely needed, and, increasingly, on luxuries. In subsistence cultures, the focus is on necessities: food, clothing, and shelter. It could be argued that in contemporary America we have both—consumer cultures at the top of the economic ladder and subsistence cultures at the very bottom—though this may be stretching things a bit.

The development of consumer cultures has a global dimension now. Most societies are consumer cultures, even in the third world. I can recall a recent visit to Sapa in Vietnam. Living near Sapa are tribes such as the Black Hmong, who do not have a written language and are illiterate. The Hmong men are farmers; you seldom see them in the center of Sapa. The Hmong women, and especially their daughters, are always found in Sapa. They are trying to sell trinkets and other things to tourists, who come to Sapa because it is quite beautiful and because of the native tribes there. The little Hmong girls, who are all quite charming, learn to speak many languages and exist in a kind of limbo between the modern world of the tourists and the primitive world of their tribe.

According to a friend who has also been to Vietnam recently, considerable changes are taking place in the ethnic tribal groups. Many young people are abandoning their traditional costuming for blue jeans and T-shirts—signifying that they are moving into modern consumer society lifestyles.

These subsistence cultures play a relatively minor role, economically speaking, in the scheme of things. The modern world is now one where free-enterprise market capitalism has triumphed, where the passion to consume things now dominates most people. Desire is infinite; there is no point, it seems, at which people say "enough" and lose their desire to make more money and buy more things.

YOU CAN BUY AS YOU PLEASE, BUT YOU CANNOT PLEASE AS YOU PLEASE

This analysis draws upon the thinking of the Puritan divine Jonathan Edwards, who struggled to find a way to reconcile human freedom and the notion of an all-powerful God. He "solved" this problem by dividing human behavior into two different realms—the realm of action and the realm of choice.

Choice	Action
God determines choices.	Individual determines actions.
We cannot please as we please.	We can act as we please.
God shapes choice.	Humans act according to choice.

People, Edwards argued, can act as they please; in other words, do whatever they want. But what they want, what pleases them, is determined by God. So we can act as we please, but we cannot please as we please. This means, critics have suggested, that human beings have only the illusion of freedom; for if God determines what pleases us, we are not really free.

In more modern terms we could say, "We can buy as we please, but we cannot please as we please," or "determine what pleases us." This means that ultimately, our actions are determined by God—or, in consumer cultures, by advertising agencies, the media, and popular culture, which have shaped or perhaps even "determined" what pleases us. We may "want what we want when we want it"; but God or the advertising agencies have determined, so this argument goes, what it is that we want. We are then, according to this argument, merely instruments of divine will or brilliant—and in all too many cases, not-so-brilliant—advertising.

Let me move to a slightly different perspective on consumer choice, namely, the arguments made about consumption in postmodern society. You will see that at least one postmodernist sociologist, Jean Baudrillard, suggests that there is an element of hidden compulsion in the consumption we find in postmodern societies.

POSTMODERNISM AND CONSUMER CULTURES

Postmodernism is a difficult term to define, and some philosophers and scholars believe there is no such thing. It is, these skeptics claim, whatever you want it to be; and, in essence, it is a bit of a put-on. The term suggests a period that comes after modernism (which ended approximately in 1960) and, for some, it is a philosophy that rejects modernism. A classic definition of postmodernism comes from the French scholar Jean-François Lyotard, who writes in *The Postmodern Condition: A Report on Knowledge:*

> Simplifying to the extreme, I define *postmodern* as incredulity toward meta-narratives. This incredulity is undoubtedly a product of progress in the sciences: but that progress in turn presupposes it. To the obsolescence of the metanarrative apparatus of legitimation corresponds, most notably, the crisis of metaphysical philosophy and of the university institution which in the past relied on it. The narrative function is losing its functors, its great hero, its great dangers, its great voyages, its great goal. (Lyotard 1984, xxiv)

What this suggests is that the old grand (meta) narratives—coming from, for example, religion, Marxist ideology, and philosophical thought—are no longer considered to be valid and universally applicable. They have been supplanted by a number of smaller narratives, and nobody can be certain whether these new narratives have any validity or claim to legitimacy. Many postmodern theorists, I should add, have been influenced by semiotic analysis—and focus on sign production and the hyperreality found in post-modern societies.

Jean Baudrillard, one of the most important French sociologists and postmodern theorists of the present day, has argued that there is an element of *compulsion* in all forms of consumption. He suggests that nowadays consumption must be seen as a *duty*, rather than a pleasure or a means of enjoyment. In a fascinating reversal of the Puritan ethic of hard work, now enjoyment and consumption are the required "business" of the typical person, who is, so to speak, forced to have fun.

As Baudrillard explains in *The Consumer Society: Myths and Structures:*

> There is no question for the consumer, for the modern citizen, of evading this enforced happiness and enjoyment, which is the equivalent in the new ethics

of the traditional imperative to labour and produce. Modern man spends less and less of his life in production within work and more and more of it in the *production* and continual innovation of his own needs and well-being. He must constantly see to it that all his potentialities, all his consumer capacities are mobilized. If he forgets to do so, he will be gently and insistently reminded that he has no right not to be happy. It is not, then, true that he is passive. He is engaged in—has to engage in—continual activity. . . . Hence the revival of a *universal* curiosity. . . . You have to try *everything*, for consumerist man is haunted by the fear of "missing" something, some form of enjoyment. You never know whether a particular encounter, a particular experience (Christmas in the Canaries, eel in whiskey, the Prado, LSD, Japanese-style lovemaking) will not elicit some "sensation." It is no longer desire, or even "taste," or a specific inclination that are at stake, but a generalized curiosity, driven by a vague sense of unease—it is the "fun morality" or the imperative to enjoy oneself, to exploit to the full one's potential for thrills, pleasure or gratification. (Baudrillard 1998, 80)

There is almost a Calvinist cast to this analysis, except that where Calvin wanted people to attend to their souls, Baudrillard reminds us that people in postmodern societies must conscientiously pursue a life of consumption. There is a disquieting and somewhat unpleasant imperative operating here, which may explain a sense of unease some people feel when they find themselves drawn into obligatory purchasing scenarios during Christmas and certain other time periods. Notice the list that Baudrillard offers us—a trip to the Canaries, visiting the Prado museum, using LSD, drinking a certain kind of whiskey, and making love "Japanese style." They are all, it turns out, consumer activities of one sort or another.

In the postmodern lifestyle, identities are infinitely changeable and all require the consumption of products to generate the desired identity or image, and since constant identity change is now seen as normal, constant consumption is now required. It could be argued that rather than "liberating" us from the old metanarratives and the idea of a stable identity, postmodernism actually enslaves us, forcing us into a life of constant consumption in order to generate new images that form the basis of our constantly changing new identities.

The pastiche seems to be a dominant metaphor for postmodernism— mixing different genres together. We see this in postmodern buildings that combine different styles and in "fusion" cuisines in restaurants, in which, for example, French and Japanese styles of cooking are combined. What postmodernism does for consumers is enable them to put together all kinds of different combinations of housing styles, furniture, paintings, clothes

styles, and lifestyles—all of which are tied, in the final analysis, to consumption. In postmodern societies, consumers are now "liberated," and
buying anything and everything is fine because anything goes with everything else.

SUMMARY

Let me summarize some important points that I've made in my analysis
of consumption and consumer cultures in this chapter. First, I have suggested that there is an unconscious sacred or religious dimension behind
consumption—one that justifies the act of consuming as something good,
something sanctioned by God. Calvin argued that we should make use of
God's blessings. Let me repeat those important lines that Calvin wrote.
We must, he argues, avoid "that inhuman philosophy which, allowing no
use of the creature but what is absolutely necessary, not only malignantly
deprives us of the lawful enjoyment of the Divine beneficence, but which
cannot be embraced 'til it has despoiled man of all his senses, and reduced
him to a senseless block" (quoted in Van Tassel and McAharen 1969, 13).
Calvin also warned about the opposite extreme, intemperance—that is,
too much consumption. In this respect, he anticipated many of the criti-
cisms made by those who feel that personal consumption has gotten out
of hand.

Weber argued that capitalism is based, in large part, on the mind-set
produced by the Protestant ethic. He also lamented that our "care for external goods" had become an iron cage and that our passion for consumption and love of material goods had gained "an inexorable power over the
lives of men." Emerson once wrote that "things are in the saddle and ride
mankind." This statement should be modified to read "things we buy,"
many culture critics would suggest.

Mary Douglas, with her grid-group typology, argues that social relationships are the determining factor in consumption preferences and that it is
our membership in one of the four consumer cultures or lifestyles, each of
which is antagonistic to all the others, that is behind our choices. Shopping,
she reminds us, is "agonistic"—an attempt to determine not who we are,
but who we are not. This is because a person's consumer culture identity
(like concepts in Saussure's analysis) is differentially defined. This may
seem to be a tongue twister, but, as Saussure's theories suggest, *we know
who we are by knowing who we are not.*

Finally, the postmodernists argue that the old rules and beliefs that sustained our behavior no longer apply. We live in chaotic times in which people switch their identities around endlessly, it seems. In this postmodern world there is a subliminal and constant pressure on people to consume. It can be suggested that, beneath the seeming randomness and chaos of postmodernist thought and the societies postmodernism creates, there lies a unifying passion for the dollar and the euro.

By addressing individuals always as potential customers, and so attributing to them *a priori* a social identity firmly linked to that role, advertising builds the standpoint of consumption into the design of its every text. Partly under the influence of advertising, this standpoint has even become a powerful ideological force in its own right: an apolitical egalitarianism which, in disregard of differential wealth and power, is grounded in our common status as consumers. In their imagistic elaborations, symbols . . . absolutize this matrix into a full vision of a world without work, without social conflict, or indeed any socially negative features at all. (1991, 35)

—**Andrew Wernick,** *Promotional Culture:*
Advertising, Ideology and Symbolic Expression

2

PROFILES IN CONSUMPTION

To understand how our consumer culture works, it's useful to know something about the distribution of wealth in the United States. The myths that have dominated our thinking in America suggest that America is essentially a classless (that is, all middle-class), egalitarian country, with small pockets of poverty and extreme wealth at either end of the economic spectrum. This never was the case; and it certainly is not the case now, when differences among the classes have grown increasingly wide. All men (and now women) in the United States may be created equal in terms of their rights, as the Declaration of Independence asserts, but the families into which they are born and their "life chances," as the sociologists put it, are most certainly not the same.

WEALTH OF THE TOP 1 PERCENT OF AMERICAN HOUSEHOLDS

In recent years, those at the top of the economic pyramid in the United States have seen their share of the wealth increase. Fifteen years ago, the situation was bad, and since then it has gotten worse. Let me offer some statistics for 1989 and for 1998 dealing with the amount of wealth of American households:

Households	1989	1998
Top 1%	31% of total net worth	38% of total net worth
Next 9%	35% of total net worth	33% of total net worth
Bottom 90%	33% of total net worth	29% of total net worth

Source: www.federalreserve.gov/pubs/oss/oss2/about.html.

These statistics, when broken down, show that the top 1 percent of American households (approximately 835,000 households) had these characteristics:

- Greater net worth than the 90 percent of households (84 million households)
- $5.7 trillion in net worth (the 90 percent had $4.8 trillion)
- Owned 49 percent of all publicly held stock
- Owned 62 percent of all business assets
- Owned 45 percent of real estate (nonresidential)

The richest 1 percent of families owned 31 percent of the total net worth of American families in 1989 and 38 percent in 1998, which shows that economic inequality has been increasing steadily. What's interesting is that the next 9 percent (below the richest 1 percent) has seen its share of total net worth decreasing. Net worth for this group was 35 percent in 1989 and 33 percent in 1989. Thus, as early as 1989, the middle classes found themselves getting squeezed by the increasing wealth of the top 1 percent and losing ground. Data for 2004 would show an increasing disparity between the top 1 percent of American households, the next 9 percent, and the bottom 90 percent.

THE HIGHER-INCOME DELUSION

Many economists, when they deal with socioeconomic classes, focus their attention on salaries instead of wealth. The way most middle-class families survive nowadays is by having two wage earners; it is the working wives who allow many (if not most) middle-class American households to remain in the middle classes. And that is because wages, for large numbers of workers, have not gone up as fast as the cost of living. In fact, the middle classes

CONSUMER CULTURE FACTOID

In 2001, the net worth (assets minus debts) of the typical American household was approximately $86,000. Between 1998 and 2001, median net worth grew 10 percent overall but by 69 percent for the wealthiest 10 percent of American households (from roughly $492,000 to $833,000).

From www.newstrategist.com/HotTrends/archive.cfm/01-1-03.htm.

are shrinking; some social critics have suggested that America is on the way to becoming "a banana republic," with a small group of people owning almost everything and living luxuriously and the rest of the people owning very little and merely scraping by.

What I call the "higher-income delusion" refers to the fact that while many workers may have larger salaries than they had in previous years, these salaries buy less than they used to. So, many American workers are now worse off than they were in earlier years, and in many—if not most—American families, the children face the possibility of not living as well as their parents. The so-called American Dream now seems, more than ever, a fantasy rather than a possibility. The American Dream suggests that upward mobility is not only possible but probable—if one is willing to work hard and has the requisite determination and willpower. And while many people have been able to move from working-class to middle-class income levels, and sometimes even to the upper class, for most people in America the American Dream is, sadly, just that—a dream.

Let me sketch out a chart that shows the difference between our upper-class and middle- to lower-class lifestyles.

Top 1 Percent	Bottom 90 Percent
38 percent of net worth	29 percent of net worth
Luxury consumption	Necessity consumption
Travel, leisure, education	Food, housing, apparel, medical care, etc.
Professions	Trades
Elite universities	Community colleges, trade schools
Medical insurance	No medical insurance
Thin	Obese
Caucasian, Asian	Other people of color

This chart is oversimplified and somewhat hypothetical, but it is a fairly accurate sketch of the situation in contemporary America, where the split between the "haves and have-nots" is increasingly large. There are, of course, many people of color and working-class people who become middle class or even wealthy; but as a rule, the class divisions are considerable, and class differences shape consumption and many other aspects of life in America.

Fifty years ago, the sociologist W. Lloyd Warner argued that America was not a classless society but, in fact, had six socioeconomic classes, which he described as follows:

Class	Percentage of Population
upper-upper	1.4 percent
lower-upper	1.6 percent
upper-middle	10 percent
lower-middle	28 percent, common man and woman level
upper-lower	33 percent, common man and woman level
lower-lower	25 percent

For Warner, the lower-middle and upper-lower classes formed what can be described as the "common man and woman" level of American society, accounting for 61 percent of the population. They are the great consuming classes based on volume, and much of their consumption is used for necessities rather than luxuries. There are three main classes: upper, middle, and lower, and considerable differences between members of the upper and lower categories.

It is the upper-upper and lower-upper classes, and some upper-middle classes, that have the most discretionary income. They spend most of the money spent in America for luxuries such as expensive cars, jewelry, large homes, and Ivy League educations for their children. Although Warner's typology is fifty years old, it is still fairly accurate; though it probably underestimates the wealth and power of the approximately 850,000 upper-upper households, who form the top 1 percent of American families and own more wealth than the bottom 90 percent.

In 2001, the most recent year for which data is available, the distribution of wealth in the United States was approximately:

Top 1 percent of population	33 percent
Next 9 percent of population	33 percent
Bottom 90 percent of population	33 percent

A small group of people, in the upper 1 percent of the population, owns as much wealth as the bottom 90 percent of the population, showing that wealth in America is highly skewed, and the wealthiest people are becoming richer as the poorest people become poorer.

PSYCHOGRAPHICS AND CONSUMPTION

Consumption breaks down according to socioeconomic class, as well as to a number of psychographic factors, involving the values and mind-sets of consumers, and demographic factors, such as ethnicity, race, gender, place (region), and age of consumers. I have considered many of these matters in some detail in my book, *Ads, Fads, and Consumer Culture*. Here I will deal only with a comparison of different ways of categorizing consumers from a psychographic perspective; later, I will describe a number of demographic analyses.

The following chart from *Ads, Fads, and Consumer Culture*, my book on advertising, represents a compendium I made of various psychographic and demographic typologies. The VALS1 and VALS2, Yankelovich, Teenagers, and Roper-Starch lists are psychographic categories. VALS stands for Values and Life Styles and represents ways of understanding the psyches of different kinds of consumers. Marketers display a genius for putting people into categories based on their psyches or certain demographic features. The ZIP Codes list is demographic in nature, tying various categories to ZIP codes that reflect different socioeconomic classes and distinctions in the things the different classes consume.

This chart has to be read vertically. Each column lists different categories of consumers. Thus there is no similarity between survivors in VALS1 and actualizers in VALS2. It is interesting to see how the different systems classify some 200 million adult Americans; and how 30 or 40 million teenagers are characterized in the Teenagers typology; and how the Roper-Starch system, which claims to be universal, classifies some 3 billion adult human beings.

As I explained in *Ads, Fads, and Consumer Culture:*

> One generalization that emerges from the list is that certain people are trendsetters or opinion leaders and others, who form the majorities, who imitate and follow the trendsetters. And there are various other subcategories, depending on the typology, of those who fit on various rungs of the ladder below

Marketing Typologies Compared

VALS I	VALS2	ZIP Codes	Yankelovich	Teenagers	Roper-Starch
Survivors	Actualizers	Blue Bloods	Home Engineers	Influencers	Strivers
Sustainers	Fulfilleds	Money and Brains	Real Guys	Edge Group	Devouts
Belongers	Achievers	Single City Blues	Ethnic Pewneps	Conformers	Altruists
Emulators	Experiencers	Urban Gold Coast	Information Grazers	Passives	Intimates
Achievers	Believers	Bohemian	Armchair Adventurers	Integrateds	Fun Seekers
I-Am-Me's	Strivers	Young Influentials	Pools and Patios		Creatives
Experientials	Makers	Two More Rungs			Hispanics Mix
Societally Conscious	Strugglers	Gray Power			

that of the trendsetters, opinion leaders, creatives—what you will. There are some who have opted out of the system and are very hard for marketers to reach, such as the integrateds and others who follow the trendsetters and purchase things to generate an image of success.

Some of the typologies, such as the Yankelovich one, don't seem to be directly involved with fashion and such, but the magazines people in the various categories read suggest these people are motivated by the same things as those in categories more directly related to marketing.

We can also see various oppositions in these typologies:

Actives	Passives
Leaders	Followers
Creatives	Imitators
Achievers	Strugglers
Influencers	Conformists
Experience seekers	Safety seekers

These polarities reflect the way the human mind functions. According to the Swiss linguist Ferdinand de Saussure, concepts are by nature differential—and our minds find meaning by setting up paired oppositions. (Berger 2004)

This set of polarities attempts to find common elements in all the other marketing typologies I dealt with, reducing consumers in all countries into two kinds of people whose psyches contrast with one another on six different topics. In the final analysis, psychographic theorists argue that it is psychological factors that can be broken down into certain groupings of types of people that ultimately shape consumer behavior.

DEMOGRAPHICS AND CONSUMPTION

In this section I will discuss the consumption practices of several important demographic groups. In a sense, I have already dealt with demographics in my analysis of the grid-group typology and its argument that there are four important lifestyles or consumer cultures in the United States and other first-world countries. Mary Douglas has argued that group affiliation with one of these consumer cultures is the determining factor in personal consumption. We can look upon her four consumer cultures as being macrodemographic groupings.

But demographers tend to look for smaller groups of people, whom they generally describe with catchy names. The list of categories of people under ZIP codes in the chart on marketing typologies is an example of this. Due to the changes that have taken place in American society in recent decades, demographers have discarded many of the categories they once used and adopted new ones that better reflect American society. A new typology called PRIZM, by the Claritas Corporation, offers some sixty-six different categories of consumers in the United States, grouped under fourteen larger categories. These fourteen major categories, connected to lifestyles and income, are:

	LIFESTYLES			
	Urban	Suburban	Second City	Town & Country
	Urban Uptown	Elite Suburbs	Second City Society	Landed Gentry
I N C O M E	Midtown Mix	The Affluentials	City Centers	Country Comfort
	Urban Cores	Middle Blurbs	Micro City Blues	Middle America
	Inner Suburbs	Rustic Living		

Source: www.cluster1.claritas.com/MyBestSegments/Default.jsp?ID=51 (accessed January 2, 2004).

CONSUMER CULTURE FACTOID

In 2002, almost 25 percent of working wives earned more money than their husbands did.

From www.newstrategist.com/HotTrends/archive.cfm/05-1-03.htm.

Claritas explains how PRIZM, which was originally devised twenty years ago, works:

> PRIZM operates on the principle that "birds of a feather flock together." It's a worldwide phenomenon that people with similar cultural backgrounds, needs, and perspectives naturally gravitate toward one another, choose to live in neighborhoods offering affordable advantages and compatible lifestyles. That's why, for instance, many young career singles and couples choose dynamic urban neighborhoods like Chicago's Gold Coast, while families with children prefer the suburbs which offer more affordable housing, convenient shopping, and strong local schools.

Claritas, which obtains its material by using data from the U.S. Census, augmented by survey data, argues that its material "should be interpreted as a general characterization of the population and its lifestyles, not as an exact analysis." Claritas points out that while it provides five PRIZM clusters with a given ZIP code, as many as twenty of these clusters may be included in one ZIP; and that it deals with likelihoods of purchasing preferences, not actual behavior.

Claritas's "You Are Where You Live" was created at the ZIP code level, each of which covers approximately 2,500 to 15,000 households; but PRIZM actually deals with census block groups (around 250–500 households) and ZIP+four (around 6–12 households). The smaller the number of homes it deals with, Claritas points out, the more precise its information. If Claritas is right, it means that it knows, with a fair degree of confidence, a great deal about the consumer behavior of all the households in a block area of six to twelve households—which, if you think about it, is pretty amazing.

We have to realize that every time we purchase something with a credit card, or use a grocery card to get bargains at supermarkets, those stores obtain information about our purchasing behavior. And that information is eventually obtained by marketing research organizations.

I checked my **ZIP** code with Claritas and discovered five groups living in it: "Movers and Shakers," "Upper Crust," "Executive Suites," "Blue Blood Estates," and "Pools and Patios." Claritas describes "Upper Crust" as follows:

The nation's most exclusive address, Upper Crust is the wealthiest lifestyle in America—a haven for empty-nesting couples over 55 years old. No segment has a higher concentration earning over $200,000 a year or possessing a postgraduate degree. And none has a more opulent standard of living.

LIFESTYLE TRAITS
Spend $3000+ foreign travel
Contribute to **PBS**
Read *Architectural Digest*
Watch *Wall Street Week*
Drive a Lexus ES300

(www.cluster1.claritas.com/MyBestSegments/Content/ Segments/demographics.jsp?)

What this cluster doesn't deal with is the fact that I bought my house thirty-five years ago, when it sold for about one-thirtieth of what it's worth on today's market. The same applies to many of my neighbors, who are, as real estate agents put it, "grandfathered in."

According to Michael Weiss, author of *The Clustering of America:*

We're no longer a country of 50 states but of 40 lifestyle clusters. . . . You can go to sleep in Palo Alto and wake up in Princeton, NJ, and nothing has changed except the trees. The lifestyles are the same. Perrier is in the fridge, and people are playing tennis at three times the national average. (Weiss 1988)

Following are some of Weiss's other clusters:

Young Influentials	Two More Rungs	Pools and Patios
New Beginnings	Gray Power	Furs and Station Wagons
New Melting Pot	Downtown Dixie-Style	Black Enterprise
Heavy Industry	Levittown, USA	Hispanic Mix
Public Assistance	Small-Town Downtown	

Businesses are marketing more and more goods and services directly to children, bypassing their parents as the target shoppers.

Weiss suggests that marketers, one day, may move beyond ZIP codes to specific mailing addresses. As he points out:

> Right now, Americans are bombarded with 15,000 messages a day. Marketers keep trying to match that little clustering niche that's your lifestyle with whatever they're trying to sell you. People leave a paper trail of warranties and subscriptions. Pretty soon Big Brother will know what's going on in your household. It's only a matter of time until businesses get into the black box of what's in a consumer's head. (Weiss 1988)

Weiss's book is a popularization of the typology developed by Claritas, which, as mentioned, uses ZIP codes to classify 250,000 neighborhoods in America into the forty consumer clusters that Weiss writes about. Now, in 2004, Claritas has expanded and refined its list of categories of consumers into sixty-six different clusters. These clusters are found in the chart that follows.

Claritas 66 Consumer Cultures

01. Upper Crust	23. Greenbelt Sports	45. Blue Highways
02. Blue Blood Estates	24. Up-and-Comers	46. Old Glories
03. Movers & Shakers	25. Country Casuals	47. City Startups
04. Young Digerati	26. The Cosmopolitans	48. Young & Rustic
05. Country Squires	27. Middleburg Managers	49. American Classics
06. Winner's Circle	28. Traditional Times	50. Kid Country, USA
07. Money & Brains	29. American Dreams	51. Shotguns & Pickups
08. Executive Suites	30. Suburban Sprawl	52. Suburban Pioneers
09. Big Fish, Small Pond	31. Urban Achievers	53. Mobility Blues
10. Second City Elite	32. New Homesteaders	54. Multi-Culti Mosaic
11. God's Country	33. Big Sky Families	55. Golden Ponds
12. Brite Lites, Li'l City	34. White Picket Fences	56. Crossroads Villagers
13. Upward Bound	35. Boomtown Singles	57. Old Milltowns
14. New Empty Nests	36. Blue-Chip Blues	58. Back Country
15. Pools & Patios	37. Mayberry-ville	59. Urban Elders
16. Bohemian Mix	38. Simple Pleasures	60. Park Bench Set
17. Beltway Boomers	39. Domestic Duos	61. City Roots
18. Kids & Cul-de-Sacs	40. Close-In Couples	62. Hometown Retired
19. Home Sweet Home	41. Sunset City Blues	63. Family Thrifts
20. Fast-Track Families	42. Red, White, & Blues	64. Bedrock America
21. Gray Power	43. Heartlanders	65. Big City Blues
22. Young Influentials	44. New Beginnings	66. Low-Rise Living

I should point out that some researchers take issue with the notion that "you are where you live" and other demographic factors. They use other indicators—such as magazines people read—to deal with consumer behavior, just as some marketing researchers put more faith in psychographic factors, involving values and beliefs of consumers.

Children as Consumers

An article in the December 18, 2003, issue of the *New York Times* had an interesting headline and subhead:

The Client Is Refined, Picky, and 3 Feet Tall
Children are making the decisions on bedroom decor.

It dealt with the fact that young children are now making decisions about how their rooms are to be decorated, thanks to marketing by companies like Pottery Barn, which has a teen catalog and seventy-eight Pottery Barn Kids stores. Pottery Barn and a number of other companies selling furniture and other products now bypass parents and appeal directly to children.

As the U.S. population grows more diverse and as immigrants move up the economic ladder, race and ethnicity are becoming less important than education, income, home ownership, age and lifestyles. In fact, as Hispanics, blacks and Asian-Americans increasingly move into middle-class suburbs and prosperous neighborhoods, they're more identified by their lifestyles and spending habits than by their ancestry.

Marketing experts have caught on to this and other dramatic changes in American life since 1990: record immigration, aging, suburban sprawl and rising numbers of singles, single parents and households without kids.

To reflect the demographic shifts, they've overhauled the catch labels they use to define the population clusters that retailers, advertisers and government agencies want to reach.

"The two great forces, aging and diversity, have rendered the traditional categories in many cases irrelevant," says Robert Lang, director of the Metropolitan Institute at Virginia Tech. . . . The research brain trusts are pinpointing who lives where; what they're most likely to read, drive and eat; how many kids they have; and where they shop. And they're doing it with unprecedented precision. They are going far beyond the characteristics of people in certain ZIP codes to details about people in specific neighborhoods—even individual households.

Haya El Nasser and Paul Overberg, "Old Labels Just Don't Stick in 21st Century," *USA Today,* December 17, 2003, p. 17A.

What many marketers are interested in now is "capturing the minds of our children," to quote the title of an article in the December 14, 2003, *San Francisco Chronicle.* The article is actually an editorial and part of a series of editorials the paper is running on the commercialization of childhood. It discusses a marketing conference, held at Harrah's Casino in Las Vegas, that focused its attention on getting into the minds of kids:

That essentially was the theme of a two-day gathering this month where leading marketers of product to children met to pass on their ideas on how to pry loose kids' consumer dollars—and, equally important, those of their parents.

The editorial mentions that the conference was sponsored by Kid Power Xchange, a subsidiary of the International Quality and Productivity Center, which hosts many such contests and is increasingly getting into the business of marketing to children. The editorial continues:

> Especially alluring are "tweens," the 8- to 12-year-olds who spend $100 million of their money each week, and influence parents to spend billions more.
> We have nothing against creative use of the free-market system. But in the battle for their pocketbooks, parents and children are at a huge disadvantage against a potent amalgam of sophisticated advertising techniques mixed with the latest insights into child development.

The editorial includes a quotation by two scholars, Diane Levin and Susan Linn, from a book titled *Psychology and the Consumer Culture.* There, Levin and Linn assert that "growing evidence documents marketing's negative effects on children's physical, psychological, and social well-being."
Although we continually say how much we value childhood, large numbers of marketers and advertisers feel it is perfectly acceptable to exploit children's innocence, naïveté, and psychological needs—and their well-known "pester power"—to sell them products and services.

Targeting Tweens

In the United States, there are something like 25 million tweens—children in the 8- to 12-year-old age group (some put tweens in the 8- to 14-year-old group)—who are of consummate interest to marketers. That's because they have spending money of their own, because they influence decisions made

---

MAKING MONEY OFF OF THE IDS OF KIDS

The Kid Id Study, based on a survey of four thousand 8- to 14-year-olds, helps "feed into core needs, wants, wishes, and fears of your target audience," as well as "identify unmet youth needs for the creation of new products and services," according to its promotional material. Cost: $30,000.

San Francisco Chronicle, December 14, 2003, p. D-4.

by their parents about purchases, and because if they can be "captured" by companies selling products they will use in the future, they will be a great source of revenue. On July 29–30 in 2002, a conference titled "Targeting Tweens" was held in New York. The following Internet ad was used to publicize the conference:

Marketing to the In BeTWEEN States
They're 10 going on 16 . . . not kids, not teens . . . they're Tweens. Viewing themselves as sophisticated and mature, they have an attitude that's all their own. Tweens have become one of the nation's most significant consumer groups. Huge amounts of music, television, movies, games, electronics, fashion and food are being marketed in their direction—and they're buying. **Spending by U.S. Tweens will reach nearly 41 Billion in 2005.** (www.iirusa.com/tweens/; accessed August 5, 2002)

So children 8 to 12 (or 14) now are "targeted" to be recruited and exploited by marketers. An article on the Internet published by the Media Awareness Network explains:

A 2000 report from the Federal Trade Commission in the U.S. revealed how Hollywood routinely recruits tweens (some as young as nine) to evaluate its story concepts, commercials, theatrical trailers and rough cuts for R-rated movies. By treating pre-adolescents as independent mature consumers, marketers have been very successful in removing the gatekeepers (parents) from the picture—leaving tweens vulnerable to potentially unhealthy messages about body image, sexuality, relationships and violence. (www.media-awareness.ca/english/parents/marketing/issues_teens_marketing.cfm; accessed July 14, 2002)

CONSUMER CULTURE FACTOID

Approximately 60 percent of 12th graders have had sexual intercourse. The majority of Americans between 18 and 49 have used illicit drugs. Some 33 percent of babies in America are born out of wedlock.

From www.newstrategist.com/HotTrends/archive.cfm/12-1-02.htm (accessed March 2004).

What is happening, I would suggest, is that marketers and advertising agencies, aided by insights gained from psychologists, are waging a war on childhood and destroying it, to the extent that they can, so that children can be turned into consumers. Childhood has been turned into training for the endless consumption found in adolescence and beyond.

If tweens are "10 going on 16," as the "Targeting Tweens" conference suggests, it means our children are prematurely older and have lost a great deal of their childhood—an important period for their psychological development. During the Middle Ages, a child was generally thought to be a small adult. In our postmodern society, we have turned children into small adults—in relation to their consumption practices, that is. Their desire to be "cool" forces them onto a consumption treadmill, for when large numbers of tweens adopt certain cool items of fashion, or whatever, those things that are no longer cool must be abandoned and they have to find something else. The process goes on endlessly.

Teenager Consumption in the United States

Let me conclude this discussion of the demographic aspects of consumer behavior with a case study on teenagers and their purchasing practices. A

CONSUMER CULTURE FACTOID

Preteen girls are a major market unto themselves. Marketers use the term *tweens* to describe the 20+ million children aged 8–14 who spend 14 billion euros a year on clothes, CDs, movies and other "feel-good" products. Limited Too sells mostly to 10- and 11-year-old girls and now mails a catalogue directly to preteen girls rather than to their parents. Not surprising, since preteen girls buy over $4.5 billion of clothing a year. Limited Too is developing makeup products targeted at this age segment as well, featuring fragrances like Sugar Vanilla and Snow Musk.

Michael Solomon, Gary Bamossy, and Soren Askegaard, 2002. *Consumer Behavior: A European Perspective*, 2nd ed. (Harlow, England: Financial Time Prentice-Hall), 411.

CONSUMER CULTURE FACTOID

In 2003 there were around 31 million teenagers in the United States, who spent some $150 billion of their own money. In 2010 there should be around 35 million teenagers in the United States.

From www.teenresearch.com/NewsView.cfm?edit_id=60.

---

good deal of this material was taken from the Claritas and New Strategist sites on the Internet, though I've also relied on material from other sources, such as the *New York Times, USA Today*, and other newspapers.

In 2002, according to a 2003 release from Teen Research Unlimited (TRU), there were an estimated 32 million teenagers (ages 12 to 19) in the United States, who spent $170 billion. This shows a significant gain from 2000, when they spent $155 billion. According to TRU, "teen consumers spent an average of $101 per week last year. This spending total combines teens' own discretionary spending and any spending they do on their parents' behalf, whether for personal or household purchases" (www.teenresearch.com/Prview.cfm?edit_id=152; accessed January 2, 2004). That means the average teenager spends approximately $5,300 a year. Teenagers get this money from their parents, part-time jobs, gifts, and odd jobs. Teen Research Unlimited obtained its information from a nationally representative survey of teenagers and by polling thousands of focus groups.

And what are these teenagers buying? Until fairly recently, they spent their money on clothes; but this seems to be changing. In a *New York Times* article dated December 2, 2003 ("Clothing Retailers Struggle to Size Up Teenagers," p. C6), author Tracie Rozhon quotes Marshall Cohen, an analyst with the NPD Group (a consulting firm for retailers), who suggests that teenagers now spend money on "cell phones, digital cameras, video games and music. Teenagers are no longer the driving category in clothes." Rozhon also quotes Greg Weaver, the chief executive of Pacific Sunwear, who says, "Teenagers are very fickle. Items are either hot or very cold."

According to Peter Zollo, author of *Wise Up to Teens*, there is a segmentation system for teens that breaks down as follows:

Edge   11 percent (outsiders)
Influencers   10 percent (embrace fashion trends early)

Conformers   44 percent (insecure, follow lead of influencers)
Passives   35 percent (not interested in fitting in)

It's the "edge" teenagers who start many of the trends. They are the ones who researchers believe started trends such as skateboarding, body piercing, tattoos, bizarre hair coloring, and a taste for alternative music. These edge teenagers are passionate about music and tend to live for the moment.

In 2002, many teens were asked to fill out a Coolest Brand Meter. The results were as follows (www.newstrategist.com/HotTrends/; accessed February 2004):

1. Nike
2. Sony
3. Abercrombie & Fitch
4. Adidas
5. Pepsi
6. American Eagle
7. Old Navy
8. Coca-Cola
9. Chevrolet
10. Tommy Hilfiger

A large number of teens are, so research suggests, obsessed with style and with quality; but they are also concerned about fitting in and not being seen as square. There is, we must recognize, a compulsive element to fashion. To avoid standing out and being different, large numbers of teens feel compelled to follow the lead of the "influencer" teens in fashion and the consumption of other things as well. There is, Zollo points out, a correlation between advertisements and the assessments teens make of many products. As he explains:

> Advertising is a key criterion of what constitutes a cool brand to teens. It's no surprise, then, that teens' favorite television commercials correlate with their favorite brands. When we ask teens about their favorite ads, they frequently mention ads from companies at or near the top of the cool brand list. (www.newstrategist.com/HotTrends/; accessed January 2, 2004)

We see, then, that advertising plays a considerable role in shaping the consumer consciousness of teens as well as other age groups. As the following chart shows, today's teenagers are members of Generation Y. They were born in the later years of that category—in the late 1980s and early 1990s.

Generations	Years
World War II	before 1933
Swing	1933–1945
Baby Boomers	1946–1964
Generation X	1965–1976
Generation Y (Millennials)	1977–1994
Not named yet	1994–

Teenage spending, because so much of it is discretionary and based on allowances, gifts, odd jobs, and part-time labor, does not follow economic ups and downs very closely. Still, to the extent that money from parents plays a role in teenager spending, cycles in the economy must have some effect on teenager patterns of consumption. TRU lists some teenage trends of interest, shown in the following chart:

Down	Up
Baggy clothes	Sunglasses (worn indoors)
Funky nail polish colors	Kickboxing
Used jeans	Girls' snowboarding clothes
Coffeehouses	Swing music

The American high school, where we find teens trying to find an identity and fighting their battles—between "innies" and "outies" for popularity, influence, and whatever else—is full of cliques. In one of my classes several years ago, I asked my students to list some of the cliques found in their schools. Here is the resulting composite list of high school cliques, whose names express their meaning quite well.

White punks on dope	Skateboarders	Preppies
Greasers	Jocks	Cheerleaders
Nerds	Hoods	Musicians
Dorks	Dweebs	Goths

These cliques help students find companionship and are the functional equivalent, one might surmise, of the ZIP codes that marketing demographers find so interesting. In their high schools, as well as in their ZIP codes, birds of a feather also flock together.

CONSUMER CULTURE FACTOID

According to a report in the February 2004 issue of *USA To-day*, the hit TV series *American Idol* is now being turned into a brand. As journalist Bill Keveney writes,

> First came books and music related directly to the competi-tion. Next came karaoke machines and other ways to re-create the *Idol* experience. Now the *Idol* lifestyle is being marketed. Some $45 million worth of "American Idol" products were sold in the 2003 holiday season, including perfume and body spray, sunglasses, summer clothes.

Keveney also quotes Michael Wood of Teenage Research Un-limited, who says, "If there's an emotional connection to something, they [teenagers] want all the products that go with it." Wood adds that teenagers "get bored easily and can turn quickly on a show or a product." The advantage that *Idol* has is that a new cast is introduced each season, so the teens don't get tired of seeing the same people on the show.

Bill Keveney, *USA Today,* February 2, 2004, p. D I.

NATIONALITIES AND CONSUMPTION

The statistics on the amount of money teenagers spend may be shocking to many people—especially members of the Swing generation (like myself), parents of children approaching teenager-hood, and people from foreign countries. It is useful to contrast consumption across cultures to get a sense of the importance of any statistics on consumption in America.

In an article entitled "Consuming Passions" (*Economist,* January 3, 2004), we get some information about consumption patterns in Asian coun-tries. The unnamed author of the article discusses the ideas of Suhel Seth, an executive of Equus Red Cell, an advertising agency in Delhi. Seth ex-plains that there has been a process of "yuppification" in India. (Yuppies, we must remember, are young urban professionals.) This yuppification has sig-nificantly changed Indian traditions. As we read:

> Seth . . . cites two ways in which the phenomenon [of yuppification] is chal-lenging Indian tradition. First, young people positively relish conspicuous

consumption. They do not share the qualms felt by their parents, brought up in a climate that mixed Nehruvian socialism with ancient Hindu ideals of renunciation. "Rolex," says Mr. Seth with his profession's knack for pithy hyperbole, "has replaced religion."

Second, and potentially of vast significance for a country as stratified as India, this is bringing about a "second unification," in which the young and affluent across the country define themselves not just by caste, creed and language, but by a shared consumer culture, spread by television, which now reaches nearly half India's homes. As a result, spending patterns are changing.

The amount of money Indians spend on basics is falling; and the amount they spend on luxuries such as dining out, going on holidays, and that kind of thing has been rising. Lifestyles are also changing. Young people used to live at home until they were married, but that is no longer the case.

In the *Economist* article, we read about young professionals who think nothing of spending 500 rupees ($11) for a shot of imported malt whiskey, which is the amount of money a typical agricultural laborer earns in a week. A chain of Barista coffeehouses is changing tea-drinking India's notions about what kind of beverage to drink, and many new malls, multiplex cinemas, and upscale bars have been built in recent years. Seth argues that all these changes are superficial and that the "cultural DNA" of India won't change; but this conclusion, the article suggests, may not be correct.

In the same *Economist* issue, an article on China discusses a magazine called *Shanghai Tatler,* which is distributed to "new rich Chinese people who are willing to spend money on luxury items." As we read:

> In glitzy new hotels, members of the city's fast-growing rich elite are learning how to party like their counterparts in America and Europe. The dream of foreign makers of luxury goods is beginning to come true.

So, no matter where you look, you find people with lots of money spending it on various kinds of luxuries. There is, it can be said, a global cast to the development of consumer cultures; and it is spread, to a considerable degree, by the mass media—by movies, television, and videos.

SUMMARY

In this chapter I've dealt with the difference between wealth and income. It turns out that the top 1 percent of Americans own more wealth than the bottom 90 percent of Americans. And the 9 percent below this top 1 percent is finding its share of wealth slipping. Many Americans have decent salaries, and so the discrepancy between the wealth of the top 1 percent and the rest of the country is not an issue for most people. I call this situation the "higher-income delusion" and suggest that the incomes people make mask the fact that a small elite group is being favored by the government (especially when conservative Republicans are in power) at the expense of middle- and lower-class Americans.

I then discuss the psychographic approach to consumption, which locates the desire for products and services in the psyches of individuals and like-minded groups, who are given jazzy names such as "achievers" and "I-am-me's." The focus here is on values that allegedly shape behavior. This approach contrasts with the demographic approach to consumption, which focuses on attributes of people such as their age, gender, race, and ethnicity.

Next I deal with marketing to children, followed by a case study of an important demographic group, teenagers. I discuss the amount of money a typical teenager spends each week, along with various factors relating to teenage consumption. Marketers have studied teenagers carefully because this age group has so much discretionary income. Teenagers have been categorized based on certain psychological types, such as "influencers," who allegedly help determine the choices made by other teenagers, and "conformers," who look up to these influencers.

Finally, I touch briefly on "consuming passions" in India and China, to show that what we call consumer cultures are springing up all over the world. These consumer cultures are having considerable effects on the lifestyles and cultures of the countries where they are developing. Whether these changes are superficial or profound, affecting the "cultural DNA" of the countries where they are taking place, is a matter that remains open to debate.

Some measure of greed exists unconsciously in everyone. It represents an aspect of the desire to live, one which is mingled and fused at the outset of life with the impulse to turn aggression and destructiveness outside ourselves against others, and as such it persists unconsciously throughout life. By its very nature it is endless and never assuaged; and being a form of the impulse to live, it ceases only with death.

The longing or greed for good things can relate to any and every imaginable kind of good—material possessions, bodily or mental gifts, advantages and privileges; but, beside the actual gratifications they may bring, in the depths of our minds they ultimately signify one thing. They stand as proofs to us, if we get them, that we are ourselves good, and full of good, and so are worthy of love, or respect and honour, in return. Thus they serve as proofs and insurances against our fears of emptiness inside ourselves, or of our evil impulses which make us feel bad and full of badness to ourselves and others. (1964, 26–27)

—Joan Riviere, *Love, Hate, and Reparation*

The objects which surround us do not simply have utilitarian aspects; rather they serve as a kind of mirror which reflects our own image. Objects which surround us permit us to discover more and more about ourselves. (2002, 91)

—Ernest Dichter, *The Strategy of Desire*

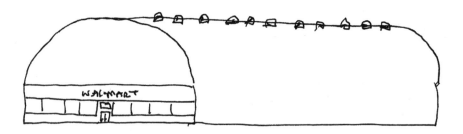

3

THE ACT OF CONSUMPTION

Let me start with psychological aspects of consumption. I discuss here some factors that I suggest are present in the minds of consumers in general and that help explain why people consume what they do. Explaining human behavior is very difficult, since there are often several different factors behind any given act by a person. I offer different perspectives on the act of consumption that may help us understand it better. This discussion makes considerable use of the work of Ernest Dichter, one of the fathers of the study of consumer motivation.

PSYCHOLOGICAL ASPECTS OF CONSUMPTION

Every time we reach out for some product at a store, or click on some key on our computer to put a product into our electronic shopping cart, we are performing an action. Buying things is always an action based, however, on various preceding events that have made us decide to take this action and buy a product.

Ernest Dichter discusses the complications involved in a choice of men's ties in *The Strategy of Desire*, but what he says can also be applied to the matter of deciding to buy a tie or anything:

The fact that you are not wearing your red tie today cannot be explained by a very simple one-two-three list of motivations. If you are a normal human being, an almost incredible number of factors exerted their influence on you, not only today but going back as far as your childhood. We must consider many conscious and unconscious factors such as the mood created by the weather and the kind of people with whom you associate, the state of your health, family relations, and so on. All these things often operate and work together in such a simple choice as that between a red or green tie. (Dichter 2002, 29)

We may ask ourselves, why did we buy this tie and not another, or why buy this product and not a different one that competes with it? Why this model and not another? Why now and not later? Why buy this product at all? Let me suggest that the act of buying something can be seen as the equivalent of the tip of an iceberg, which is just a small part of the iceberg. Most of the iceberg remains below the water, where we can't see it. This material below the water represents our unconscious, which, if Freud is correct, shapes many of our behaviors—including, I would add, the act of consuming things.

A mantra of advertising involves the formula "Attract attention, stimulate desire, and generate action." If we didn't know a product existed, we couldn't desire it. Advertising tells us about products and services and, playing upon forces in our psyches, makes us desire them. Without desire, we wouldn't act. But what is the basis of this desire? Let me suggest some possibilities.

TO BUY IS TO BE PERCEIVED

I have taken liberty with Bishop Berkeley's famous dictum "To be is to be perceived" and argue that one reason people buy things is to get others (salespeople in the first instance) to acknowledge their existence. When you buy something in a store, for a moment or so, you have an interaction with a person who acknowledges that you exist. You don't get this gratification on the Internet; though you usually do get some kind of e-mail message about the transaction that is a substitute for real-world, personal interactions.

Consumption may play into narcissistic elements in our personalities. I am talking, here, about our desire to be seen and to be found attractive. When we purchase something in a store, we generally have a momentary relationship with clerks who interact with us, recognize us as customers, and if they have been trained well, smile at us and acknowledge our existence. In certain kinds of stores, often dealing with fashion or upscale products, the clerks are hired based on their attractiveness or style, so we have the pleasure of an interaction with desirable (perhaps, latently, in a sexual manner) individuals. It might even be asserted that there is an unconscious sexual dimension to consumption: When we buy things we assert our power, and a connection can be made between financial power and sexual power, which helps explain the existence of so-called trophy wives.

SALES: SPEND AND SAVE AT THE SAME TIME

Sales enable consumers to have the best of both worlds—to spend money and save money at the same time. Because many people still harbor anxieties about wasting money, or about paying more for items than they should have, sales provide a certain amount of consolation to consumers. Yes, they are spending money for things they want or need; but no, they are not being wasteful.

With the money they save, consumers can then buy other things; and if those things are on sale, the process can continue ad infinitum. So the more you spend, the more you save. There is a kind of infinite regress set up: Spending on sales items involves saving money that can then be spent on other sales items, which involves saving more money.

Let's consider a very large purchase, a big-ticket item—an automobile. Because of the numerous "deals" that automobile companies offer purchasers, Americans have, in recent years, become conditioned to purchasing automobiles only when they are on sale—which is just about always— or when purchasers get certain bargains on interest rates and that kind of thing. When the typical American walks into an automobile salesroom, looking for a deal, the battle between the consumer and the salesperson is unequal. The salesperson has a great deal of experience in selling cars, and the consumer has relatively little experience in purchasing them.

To equalize things, some companies and organizations now supply consumers with data on the actual cost of the automobile to the dealer and on various payments automobile companies make to dealers. For example, *Consumer Reports* has a service that for twelve dollars provides all kinds of information to the automobile consumer about a specific model of an automobile, and the American Automobile Association and other groups provide similar services. With this kind of information, consumers have a chance of getting a better deal. So people who purchase automobiles are almost always looking for great deals, which is another way of saying automobiles on sale.

Many Internet sites also compare the prices of items people are considering buying, all of which helps consumers deal with anxieties they might feel about paying more for an item than they had to pay. During the various calendar-based consumption periods, numerous sales are announced. Some individuals don't care about sales and saving money on the things they wish to purchase, but they tend to be atypical. They may decide they have to have a certain model of car that is "hot" at a given moment in time, and they may even be willing to pay more than its list price. But this is not the norm.

In addition to deals, other factors are at work in the purchasing of automobiles. In *The Strategy of Desire*, Ernest Dichter explains what happened to one car company that designed a car with a blunt front end. He writes:

> Actually, what had happened was that this car manufacturer had run afoul of one of the irrational factors at work in human nature. The normal shape of a car has a lot to do with its symbolic significance, that of a penetrating instrument. It symbolizes speed and power; it has, further, in a psychological sense, considerable significance as a phallic symbol. In a sense, therefore, when the model with the blunt bonnet came on the market, it violated this symbolic significance of the shape of the car, and it was rejected by people who did not know quite why. In other words, to them it lacked a certain sense of potency and penetrating power. (Dichter 2002)

Dichter's point—that, among other things, cars are symbolically penises—might seem a bit strange. But that is because we are unaware of the power of the unconscious forces, many having a sexual dimension, in our psyches. I've often thought that part of the appeal of Jaguar automobiles is that they are very phallic.

GIVING OURSELVES THE REWARDS WE DESERVE

Many people, without necessarily recognizing what they are doing, consider their purchases to be rewards for meritorious behavior. This observation applies to various items people buy that do not fall into the necessities category but into what might be described as luxuries, both small and large. Thus, when people drink Coca-Cola, Pepsi-Cola, or any of the newer fruit-based soft drinks, they are unconsciously rewarding themselves in the same way that they might have been given a cookie or some other sweet for good behavior when they were children. The typical can of soda pop contains something like six teaspoons of sugar; so we are drinking colored, flavored, and sweetened water, in the most reductionistic sense of the term. But Coca-Cola and Pepsi-Cola have created stories of all kinds, through advertising, that in the minds of their consumers make these beverages more than simply colored, flavored, and sweetened water.

In this respect, it is pertinent to recall what Ernest Dichter, a founding father of motivational research, wrote in *The Strategy of Desire:*

Whatever your attitude toward modern psychology or psychoanalysis, it has been proved beyond any doubt that many of our daily decisions are governed by motivations over which we have no control and of which we are often quite unaware. (Dichter 2002, 12)

Dichter emphasizes that unconscious imperatives shape our behavior as consumers. We may often have "rational" arguments explaining our purchases, such as "I had a Coke because I was thirsty," but these statements are rationalizations that we use to delude ourselves. We drank that Coke or Pepsi because we wanted to be "good" to ourselves—and because we wanted to demonstrate our style and sophistication, among other things. Dichter also points out in his book (originally published in 1960) that there are other important motivations, such as the need to show creativity, behind our buying things.

CONSUMPTION AS A MEANS OF SHOWING CREATIVITY

One reason we buy things is to show others what kind of person we are, manifesting our creativity in our purchases. People are torn between a desire for products that are known and reliable and others that show imagination and style. Thus we are caught between fear of change and the embarrassment that comes from trying a new brand and the fear of boredom that results from using the same old brands.

CONSUMER CULTURE FACTOID

In 2003, the average American consumed 51 gallons of soft drinks a year—an average of 1.5 cans per day. Some 64 percent [of Americans] are overweight and 30 percent are obese. Per capita coffee consumption has fallen 23 percent since 1970.

From www.newstrategist.com/HotTrends/archive.cfm/12-1-02.htm.

In *The Strategy of Desire,* Dichter explains how buying can be seen as a form of creative behavior:

> Most people like to shop. When we ask them, however, why they bought a product, the answer implies a need. A much more important aspect of buying is that it gives a person a chance to be creative. In other words, every time we go out and shop for something, we are really trying to express our own creativeness in as easy a form as possible. Our products have become more and more reliable from a technological viewpoint; a GE refrigerator is not very different from a Frigidaire, as long as I pay about the same amount of money. What I do buy, then, is the personality, the image, the size of the product and brand: what it can do for me psychologically and not just technologically.
>
> I think this factor is a very important one and should not be easily overlooked; every time we go out, we do so really to prove to ourselves that we have the power to express our innermost desires by the selection of a specific type of merchandise. (Dichter 2002, 170)

If you ask people why they bought a certain product, they will usually tell you that they needed it. Dichter suggests, on the other hand, that buying products is a means for us to express our creativity and our sense of style.

For many people, purchasing goods and services is, unfortunately, the only way they can express their creativity. One of the things that people buy, then, is the personality of the object, which is created by marketers and advertising agencies. That explains the admonition "Sell the sizzle, not the steak." It is the image that often sells the product, especially in cases (such as soda pop) in which there is no appreciable difference between products.

CONSPICUOUS CONSUMPTION AS A SIGN OF SUCCESS

One thing our purchases do for us is to show the world that we are successful and can purchase expensive cars, homes, vacations—what you will. This conspicuous consumption of status symbols helps us allay anxieties we might have about whether we are successful; it also helps us demonstrate to others that we have purchasing power, and, connected to that, all kinds of other powers, including sexual power.

That is why branding is so important. The brands have auras that are transferred to those who purchase them, which helps explain why many fashion companies plaster their logos over their handbags, T-shirts, and other items. The brands we use help us better define, for ourselves and others, our personalities and our status in society. When I was growing up in the thirties and forties, driving a Cadillac was considered a big status symbol; now, where I live (in "marvelous" Marin County), Cadillacs are considered "square" (the average age of Cadillac users was 59 a few years ago). Most people in Marin show their purchasing power by buying a Lexus, Mercedes, or BMW (Basic Marin Wheels). In addition, there is the matter of whether one purchases an entry-level or top-of-the-line car. So it's clear that all kinds of distinctions come into play in the consideration of automobiles as status symbols—and of status symbols of all kinds.

We must also remember that "success" is ultimately connected in our unconscious minds with being the recipient of God's (or a higher power's) love, which—ultimately—explains our success.

CONSUMPTION AS A DRAMATIC NARRATIVE

When we purchase something, it generally is the consequence of a feeling we have that we "need" something. Thus it can be argued that the act of consumption can be seen as the result of some narrative we are involved with— a narrative in which we convince ourselves that whatever it is that we are buying is something that will enhance our lives and those of our loved ones in some way. Sometimes we purchase things on "impulse"; but, I would suggest, it is because we feel that we have an opportunity, which may pass, to take care of some long-felt need or desire. That is, what we buy serves a variety of purposes: It will make us more attractive, it will enable us to do something we want to do, or it will reward us for meritorious conduct in the past.

Wolfgang Haug, a German social scientist, suggests that we see consumption in theatrical terms. As he explains in *Critique of Commodity Aesthetics: Appearance, Sexuality, and Advertising in Capitalist Society:*

> The exhibition of commodities, their inspection, the act of purchase, and the associated moments, are integrated into the concept of one theatrical total work of art which plays upon the public's willingness to buy. Thus the salesroom is designed as a stage, purpose-built to convey entertainment to its audience that will stimulate a heightened desire to spend. . . . This aesthetic innovation of the salesroom into a "stage for entertainment" on which a variety of commodities are arranged to reflect the audience's dreams, to overcome their reservations, and provoke a purchase, was a pioneering exercise at a time marked by a general change in the selling trend. (Haug 1971, 69)

In this excerpt, Haug is discussing the ideas of the director of a department store in Zurich. The director wrote a book, *The Key to the Consumer,* in which he explained his notions of how selling had to be made into a theatrical experience, one in which the aesthetics of the salesroom were of major importance.

In this experience the consumer is the lead actor or actress, and the act of consumption is the high point of the play. This notion ties into my suggestion that one motivation behind consumption is to be perceived. When we purchase something we are, for the moment, the "star" of a short play. We also are the producer of this theatrical event; that is, we pay for it. Shopping becomes, then, a kind of entertainment.

In a *Financial Times* article titled "Department Stores Launch Counterattack" (December 23, 2003), Lauren Foster spells out this concept of shopping as dramatic narrative in some detail. Foster quotes Peter Williams, the chief executive of Selfridges, a department store in England:

> We are trying to assault everyone's senses in as many ways as we can. We're in the entertainment business to some extent. It is not just the other retailers we are competing with. We are competing for leisure time.

As Foster writes:

> The Selfridges model, he [Williams] says, is about creating an experience that is "new, interesting and different" where the product is not the sole differentiator. The store differentiates itself on a number of levels: dedicating more space to younger fashions, hosting events, emphasizing brands, and maintaining price position by holding only two sales a year.

Williams argues that American department stores "all look the same: Very often when I'm standing in the middle of a store, I can't tell which one I'm in."

There is a large illustration for the Foster article—a photograph of the new Selfridges store in Birmingham, England. The caption is most interesting: "Shopping as an art form: Selfridges new store in Birmingham on the first night of its illumination." The "art form" in Selfridges is theater, and it is the theater of consumption that is the main genre in these consumption palaces. And we are the lead actors and actresses.

THE CHAIN OF CONSUMPTION

Sometimes when we buy something, what we buy is an end in itself. That is, there's nothing more involved in the purchase than buying the object. But in other cases there is what might be called a "chain" of consumption, in that one purchase necessitates various other purchases. For example, suppose a retired couple in Seattle decides to take a Caribbean cruise in February to escape from the nasty weather, among other things. After purchasing their cruise, they have other purchases that are made necessary by that first purchase.

They have to buy travel insurance, in case one of them becomes ill and they can't take the cruise. They also have to book flights to Miami, or to whatever city from which the cruise departs. Due to the length of the air trip, they have to arrive the day before their cruise sails, so they have to book a hotel for a night. They might buy some new clothes to wear on the cruise, especially for the formal nights, when many men wear tuxedos and women wear evening gowns. Also, they probably will feel compelled to buy gifts for their children. If they decide to take tours of the islands they visit, they have to purchase tours offered by the shipping line or tour or arrange for one on their own. Then there are various other things to buy, such as photographs taken by the ship's photographer, drinks, and perhaps dinners at special restaurants most cruise liners now have.

The following list shows the "chain" of consumption in graphic detail:

1. Purchase a cruise.
2. Purchase travel insurance.
3. Purchase round-trip airline tickets.
4. Book a night at a hotel for the night before sailing.
5. Purchase new clothes.
6. Purchase gifts for family and friends.
7. Purchase drinks and special dinners.
8. Purchase tours from shipping line or pay cabs or local people for touring.
9. Leave tips for waiters and cabin attendants at end of cruise.
10. Pay for miscellaneous expenses such as cab fare to and from the airport.

Not all of these links in the chain of consumption are necessary; but for most people, once the decision to take a cruise is made, the other decisions follow almost automatically. Some of these expenses are considerable. For example, it is customary for each passenger to pay approximately $10 per day for the services of his or her waiter, assistant waiter, and cabin steward. Thus a two-week cruise for two people costs an additional $280 in tips. This money is automatically deducted from the passenger's credit card at the end of the cruise.

MIMETIC DESIRE: IMITATING THE DESIRE OF OTHERS

The concept of mimetic desire comes from the work of a French literary theorist, René Girard, who uses it to explain Shakespeare's work in his book *A Theater of Envy: William Shakespeare*. Girard argues that what we desire is primarily based on what others desire. *Mimesis* means "imitation," so *mimetic desire* means that we imitate the desire of others—whether it is for material objects or marriage partners. According to Girard, Shakespeare's characters desire people essentially because others desire them. Girard also discusses Helen of Troy and the Trojan War; he suggests that the Greeks wanted Helen back because the Trojans had her, and the Trojans wanted to keep her because the Greeks wanted her back. The fact that these two countries fought a ruinous war over one woman suggests how powerful a force mimetic desire is.

As Girard explains:

> When we think of those phenomena in which mimicry is likely to play a role, we enumerate such things as dress, mannerisms, facial expressions, speech, stage acting, artistic creation, and so forth. Consequently, we see imitation in social life as a force for gregariousness and bland conformity through the mass reproduction of a few social models.
>
> If imitation also plays a role in desire, if it contaminates our urge to acquire and possess, this conventional view, while not entirely false, misses the main point. Imitation does not merely draw people together, it pulls them apart. Paradoxically, it can do these two things simultaneously. Individuals who desire the same thing are united by something so powerful that, as long as they can share whatever they desire, they remain the best of friends; as soon as they cannot, they become the worst of enemies. (Girard 1991, 3)

Many advertisements play upon the element of mimetic desire in our psyches by showing people who are attractive or famous using certain products. We then imitate these people, and, in particular, we imitate and desire what they have desired and purchased.

The power of identification is very strong. When we are young, we identify with various heroes and other characters from the narratives to which we have been exposed—from fairy tales, books, television programs, and films. I offered an example of this in chapter 2, in my discussion of teenagers who purchase *American Idol* products. When we are older and have purchasing power (if no other kind, to speak of), we imitate those we identify with in the only way we can—by imitating their consumption patterns.

The "Uggs" boots fad is a good example of how this works. In a *Wall Street Journal* article (January 6, 2004) titled "Deckers Shares May Have Run Right out of Their Uggs," Gregory Zuckerman writes:

> Uggs, which mostly are made in New Zealand and Australia, have been staples of the ski and surf communities for more than two decades. But they were considered gauche for urbanites until stars such as Oprah Winfrey and Gwyneth Paltrow began wearing them around town a year or so ago. Deckers began selling Uggs, notable for their furry tops, in different colors, such as pink and blue, expanding beyond black, brown and tan. By late last year they were marching off their shelves.

The Uggs fad is a good example of mimetic desire—that is, imitation—in operation and of the power of stars and celebrities to influence fashion tastes.

PLACES OF CONSUMPTION

Wolfgang Haug explains that the act of consumption is tied to the aestheticization of the selling process. As he writes in *Critique of Commodity Aesthetics: Appearance, Sexuality, and Advertising in Capitalist Society:*

> Now, when a commodity is sold, the customer not only pays for its styling and the name made famous through advertising, but also for the styling of the selling process. As far as the commodity is concerned, conscious efforts are made to shift the emphasis from the specific commodity to the experience of consumption.
>
> Ultimately the aestheticization of commodities means that they tend to dissolve into enjoyable experiences, or into the appearance of those experiences, detached from the commodity itself. . . . To establish this trend, it is not enough to mould and remould the army of sellers: one must condition the instincts and behavior of the "public at large." And since young people are the easiest to manipulate, they become the instrument and expression of a general trend towards moulding. (Haug 1971, 72)

With this insight in mind, let us consider some interesting aspects of the consumption process relative to where people buy things.

The Department Store

Since I have dealt with department stores as important and rapidly evolving sites of consumer theater, let me say something about department stores as functional alternatives to medieval cathedrals. I dealt with this topic in my book *Ads, Fads, and Consumer Culture,* and this analysis draws on that material.

Department Stores as Functional Alternatives to Cathedrals

Department Store	Cathedral
Modern	Medieval
Paradisical: Heaven on Earth now	Paradisical: Heaven in the future
Passion: Merchandising	Passion: Salvation
Sales: Save money	Prayer: Save souls
Sacred texts: Catalogs	Sacred texts: Bible, prayer books
Clerks	Clergy
Sell: Products	Sell: God
Possessions as signs of spiritual election	Holiness as a sign of spiritual election
Big sales	Religious holidays
Sale of an expensive product	Conversion of a sinner
Buy incredible gifts	Experience miracles
Pay taxes	Pay tithe
Muzac	Religious music
Lighting to sell	Lighting to inspire reverence
Bad credit	Penance
Advertising	Proselytizing
Cash register	Offering plate
Brand loyalty	Devotion

These parallels between department stores and cathedrals suggest that there is something holy, something of the sacred, connected to purchasing objects. The things we buy are signs, it can be surmised, that we have been blessed. And so we consume, often with religious fervor—even though we may not recognize the sacred dimension of our activities. The fact that the traditional department store is under attack by Wal-Mart, Target, and other discount retailers might be seen as analogous to the Protestant revolution, with new evangelical forms of worship/consumption replacing the once-dominant city-centered Roman Catholic cathedral/department store.

Some years ago I happened to be on a radio program with Stanley Marcus, who was celebrating the opening of a Neiman-Marcus department store in San Francisco. When I mentioned my hypothesis about the relationship between cathedrals and department stores, Marcus said he thought it made good sense, since the areas around medieval cathedrals were often the center of commerce. The development of new types of department stores, to counter the discount stores and other competing retailing operations, would be analogous to the Counter-Reformation—to

changes in the Catholic Church, as it reacted to competition from Protestant sects. When I suggested there were certain parallels between department stores and cathedrals, I was unaware of the writings of Emile Zola, who made the same comparison. Rachel Bowlby, in a chapter of *The Shopping Experience* titled "Supermarket Futures," writes:

> The department store is the "cathedral of modern commerce" (Xoal); and it appears as a "palace": for the middle classes, symbol of the "democratization of luxury" (Georges d'Avenel). As a palace, it affects an image of opulent leisure accessible to anyone who cares to enter and participate vicariously in an image of the aesthetically aristocratic life. As a cathedral, it takes over from religion; it has its consecrated building, and its own rituals and festive seasons (designated times for sales and events in relation to particular themes and product groups). (Bowlby 1997, 97)

I will say more later about department stores, which in many cases are now fighting for their lives.

Supermarkets and Super Drugstores

Supermarkets are places where we go to buy necessities—something to eat for ourselves and our pets—but where we often buy other things on impulse, such as magazines, flowers, toys, electronic gadgets, and even television sets and radios. The amount of money we spend in supermarkets is tied to the amount of time we spend in them, so their owners are interested in making us linger in them as long as possible.

Supermarkets are designed very carefully. Certain products, such as pet foods, are located in the interior aisles so as to draw us farther into the store. Once we are there, the retailer hopes we will purchase other products that catch our attention. Location of foods on the shelf—at eye level or below—is an important element in selling, so food manufacturers must compete to get the best placement for their products. Necessities such as dairy products, meat, fruits, and vegetables are placed on the outer aisles of the store, where access is easy. Increasingly, supermarkets also place bakeries and delicatessens along their perimeters, since they are in competition with fast-food stores for take-out foods such as sandwiches and salads. Many supermarkets also have banks and pharmacies at their perimeters.

At the same time that supermarkets are stocking nonfood items, what might be called super drugstores are increasingly stocking food items—along with electronic gadgets, watches, clothes, plants, and other items that might also be found in supermarkets. So there is a great deal of competition between supermarkets and super drugstores.

Big-Box Stores

Stand-alone supermarkets and drugstores are increasingly in competition with big-box merchandisers such as Costco and Wal-Mart, which have very large supermarket operations in addition to all the other things they sell. Since Wal-Mart doesn't pay union wages, and since it buys things in enormous quantities, it can get products at the lowest possible cost. Thanks to economies of scale, it can sell groceries (and everything else) for less than supermarkets, which means that they are all in a life-and-death struggle with Wal-Mart, Costco, and other big-box stores. Wal-Mart may be considered the 800-pound gorilla of contemporary merchandising in the United States—and, increasingly, in other countries as well.

These big-box stores—especially Wal-Mart—now threaten to dominate and overwhelm all the supermarkets, toy stores, clothes stores, liquor stores, bookstores, and many other kinds of stores in the United States and other countries. In many areas where these big-box stores locate, they have devastated the small stores around them, though there is some debate about Wal-Mart's impact. Small stores are fighting back by trying to prevent communities from letting Wal-Mart build its gigantic stores, citing the record of devastation of downtown areas in many places where they are located.

An article I accessed from the Internet, "Impact of Wal-Mart on Downtowns," offers two views of the Wal-Mart impact:

> Wal-Mart's impact on traditional downtown retailing has been startling. "As Wal-Mart rolled out its franchises, it sucked commerce off Main Streets, destroying traditional retailers that had served their communities for generations. But in the face of the abundance Wal-Mart produced, in the form of more jobs, consumer savings, and expanded trade, the loss of Main Street life seemed an incidental price to pay."[1]

> The long-term impact of Wal-Mart is less clear. Some downtown businesses in cities where Wal-Marts have located have benefited from the greater draw of customers. Others have been devastated by the overwhelming new competi-

tion for their customers' dollars. In a study of the impact of 14 Wal-Marts in Iowa, Kenneth Stone found positive impact in towns where Wal-Mart had located. However, there was clearly a negative impact on other towns in the surrounding area; towns within a 20-mile radius of the Wal-Mart stores saw total retail sales drop an average of 25 percent after five years.[2] (www.emich.edu/public/geo/557book/c313.impactwalmart.html; accessed December 28, 2003)

1. Edward O. Welles, "When Wal-Mart Comes to Town," *INC*, July 1993, 78.
2. Welles, "When Wal-Mart Comes to Town," 78.

Whether Wal-Marts are the enemies of small-town America is debatable. That these giant Wal-Mart Supercenters—some of which are 250,000 square feet in size, including full-service grocery stores—have had a major impact on nearby communities and retailers, and on the whole retailing industry, cannot be denied.

LINGUA CONSUMPTA: LINGUISTIC OBFUSCATION AND SELF-DELUSION

Our use of language helps us avoid any sense of guilt we may have about being consumers, especially luxury consumers, when so many people in America are suffering—many children are starving, and many couples cannot afford to live in an apartment or home. The critique made by many scholars and writers of our consumer society, we must remember, is a moral one.

So we have developed a way to avoid anxieties and guilt when we consume by substituting other terms for *buy* or *purchase*. Let me offer a few of them.

- *Get.* As in "I'm going to get myself a new Lexus, now that there are so many great deals around."
- *Book.* As in "I booked a weeklong cruise on the Crystal line for only $4,000 for the two of us."
- *Ordered.* As in "I ordered two new suits." This term also suggests a kind of dominance, in which the purchaser can "command" a certain thing to be done.
- *Found.* As in "I found a great dress on sale." Here the act of buying something is seen as a matter of discovery and, to some degree, luck. If we found something, there is a suggestion that it was in some way hidden. It was hidden not by being secreted away, but by being "lost" in a huge display of dresses.

- *Stole.* As in "I really stole that pair of boots from Nordstrom at their year-end sale." Here the language is a bit inflated, and the term *stole* is used to mean "I got a really fabulous bargain."

By using terms such as these, we try to delude ourselves and avoid recognizing that we are buying or consuming some object or service. This practice may be connected to a sense of guilt some people feel about consuming, or to anxiety about the amount of money they are spending relative to their income.

MODES OF CONSUMPTION

There are a limited number of ways that we can buy things, and each mode of consumption has its particular attributes and gratifications and limitations. I will deal here with buying things in person, on the telephone, by mail order, and on the Internet.

Buying Things in Person

When we buy things in person we obtain, as I suggested earlier, the "reward" of being perceived, of being spoken to, of being acknowledged as a human being. This relationship between a customer and a clerk is a formality; and in some cases, perhaps when clerks are harried or in a bad mood, it is not always satisfying. When you buy something in person, you actually have the product in hand. Sometimes, such as when you purchase shoes or clothes, you can try the product on. In addition, when buying things in person, you can browse through the store and find other items on sale.

Shopping is a form of entertainment and recreation. Many people shop for the sheer pleasure of being out and about, seeing the good things available in the world, without looking for any particular item.

Buying Things by Phone

Purchasing things by phone is one step removed from the kind of personal encounters we have when we buy something in person, at a store. Because we do have another person to talk to when buying things by phone, we get a diluted form of personal recognition and confirmation of the fact that we exist.

We buy things over the phone when we see them advertised on television, in a newspaper, or in some other publication and don't want to bother going out to search for the item in some store. In some cases, certain items are available only by being purchased over the phone or on the Internet.

Buying Things by Mail Order

Many people use mail order to purchase things. Certain industries, such as magazine publishing, make great use of the mail system to obtain subscriptions. When we buy things by mail order, we have time to reconsider our decision, so mail order introduces a bit of rationality into the equation. It also allows time for those who purchase things this way to change their mind, as "buyer's remorse" sets in.

Buying Things on the Internet

Shopping on the Internet is—or can be—the most rational means of purchasing a product. That's because you can use various websites to compare product pricing and obtain product evaluations. You don't get the gratification of interacting with a person, or of being able to touch the product (trying clothes on, for example), but you do get a wonderful sense of power as you simply click a button and purchase a product. Buying things on the Internet is tied to the credit system, for you need a credit card to make a purchase. Some people use the Internet to look up something they are contemplating purchasing. They go to various sites that evaluate the product or service; and they go to other sites that sell the product, to compare prices. Then they shut down the computer, go to a store, and buy the product in person.

Many department stores and other kinds of stores now use the Internet to sell their products and services, uniting what is called "brick" (the physical store) and "click" (the Internet store). Stores of all kinds—from Sears, Wal-Mart, and Costco to Home Depot and Victoria's Secret—are increasing their presence on the Internet; Amazon.com, the Internet virtual bookstore turned virtual Internet mall, so to speak, can be looked upon as a merchandising phenomenon. Some Internet "stores," such as Amazon.com and eBay, are virtual; they exist only on the Internet.

The eBay phenomenon is of considerable interest. In an essay, "The eBay Way: How Auction Sites Like eBay Turn Retail Economics on Its Ear for the Betterment of Just about Everybody," Robert X. Cringely explains how significant the impact of eBay has been:

> Let's put eBay in perspective. In terms of sales, the company is comparable in size to Amazon.com. But Amazon's sales are primarily composed of goods

while eBay's sales are composed almost entirely of commissions—commissions that average around five percent of the value of goods bought and sold. So while Amazon and eBay are both around a billion in sales, eBay actually represents more than $20 billion in economic activity. That makes eBay the third largest U.S. retailer after Wal-Mart and Sears, and three times the size of AOL, the other Internet merchandising powerhouse. It took Wal-Mart almost 30 years to have the economic impact eBay has reached in five years. And profits? eBay makes more profit than all the rest of the retail Internet businesses COMBINED. It is a money machine. In retail economic terms, eBay IS the Internet. (www.pbs.org/cringely/pulpit/pulpit20020725.html)

We see, then, that eBay is a marketing powerhouse—one that has turned America, and, by extension, the world, into a gigantic Internet garage sale, run by eBay and serviced by its PayPal division, which deals with payment for most purchases. Many people actually make a living by buying products

---

eBay's real significance isn't its own financial success. eBay has, more than any other company, fully harnessed the potential of the Internet. By connecting more than 30 million buyers and sellers around the world, eBay has permanently changed commerce. Things a buyer once would have spent days, weeks, or a lifetime tracking down—the rocking horse he played on as a child, the exact Buffalo nickel he needs to complete a collection—are suddenly available at any hour of the day or night, from a PC in the buyer's home. By efficiently moving goods from people who value them less to people who value them more, eBay increases "social utility," as the economists put it, making people, as a whole, happier than they would be without those goods. For sellers, eBay's impact has been just as profound. It has helped them circumvent the old order of high-priced retailing space, exclusive distribution channels, and costly advertising, and market directly to millions of buyers.

The implications of the eBay model . . . are revolutionary. eBay gives individuals a degree of economic independence that was impossible before the Internet. As many as 100,000 people are already making their living selling on eBay.

Adam Cohen, *The Perfect Store: Inside eBay* (Boston: Little, Brown, 2002), 9–10.

and selling them on eBay. And there are legions of eBay addicts, who search through eBay for just about anything they wish to buy or to sell.

Online sales in 2004 amounted to $114 billion, or, excluding travel, $71.8 billion. This $114 billion figure represents 5.4 percent of all retail sales (www.shop.org/press/04-052504.html; accessed May 25, 2004). As more Americans purchase computers and go online, given the fact that the economy seems to be rebounding, we can surmise that Americans will spend even more money on the Internet in future years.

THE CONSUMER CULTURE CALENDAR

In the United States, major periods of unusual consumption are organized around the calendar. This is not to say that people in America aren't consuming things all the time. But at certain times of the year—in many cases, holidays of one sort or another—everyone involved in selling goods and services to people makes a big push. We can distinguish, then, between ordinary consumption and what might be described as time-situated consumption.

We know, for example, that as the Super Bowl draws near, many fans purchase big-screen television sets, so they can see the game and feel closer to the action. A National Retail Federation survey suggested that 1.5 million

---

THE SUPER BOWL PIZZA CONNECTION

There's one thing that millions of Super Bowl viewers will do besides drink too much beer: gobble a slice of pizza. Or four.

Don't think the nation's pizza giants aren't aware of the cosmic link between the Super Bowl and pizza. More pizza will be sold Feb. 1, Super Bowl Sunday, than any other day of 2004. Pizza has become to Super Bowl Sunday what eggs are to Easter. Or candy canes to Christmas. . . .

"There are situations socially tied to food categories," says Jennifer Aaker, a consumer psychologist and marketing professor at Stanford University. "Just as you might go on an airplane and order a tomato juice, you watch the Super Bowl and eat pizza."

Bruce Horvitz, "Pizza People Prepare Super Bowl Blitz," USA Today, January 16, 2004, p. B1.

television sets would be sold for the 2004 Super Bowl. And these fans tend to gobble up a huge number of pizzas.

Ordinary consumption, as I will use the term, takes place when appliances wear out and have to be replaced; when people get married and have to furnish apartments and homes; when couples have children and need to buy cribs, strollers, and other things related to their new status as parents. People continually have to purchase food and pay for using their telephones, heating their homes, running their appliances, and that kind of thing.

Time-situated consumption occurs at certain times of the year, during special events (back to school) or holidays (Labor Day, Halloween, Christmas, summer vacations). At these times, there are big spurts in the consumption practices of many Americans.

Back to School

As the summer ends, not very long after people have done their summer purchasing—items such as new swimsuits, summer clothes, and suntan lotion—the back-to-school period of purchasing begins. During these months, there are sales on everything from pencils, glue, and notebooks to backpacks and clothes to computers and other electronic gizmos that modern students feel required to own.

The back-to-school shopping period is a time-situated consumer event that draws on culturally accepted ideas of what a student needs to be prepared for school.

Every fall, a huge tidal wave of students go back to school, and parents find themselves shopping for the things their children will need, or want, for their new school year. I recently saw a television program about some girls who were spending a considerable amount of money at beauty parlors on new hairdos, manicures, pedicures, and similar beauty treatments—so they would look good when they went back to high school. In addition, millions of students are either starting college or returning to college, and they need things for their dorm rooms, rooms in fraternity houses, or apartments.

The back-to-school period, like many other time-situated periods of consumption, is based on certain culturally accepted notions about what products and services are needed to function in certain situations and transition periods in life, such as going to school or moving up from grade school to middle school or from middle school to high school. Students, at younger and younger ages, have become (thanks to advertising) fashion conscious. Many insist on having only certain brands of clothes that are, for the moment, fashionable. In addition, new gadgets become popular, such as cell phones that take photographs, iPods, and other "hot" items.

Halloween

You see Halloween costumes being sold weeks, and sometimes months, before the holiday. The event originally, in modern times, was a children's holiday that enabled them to dress up in costumes—originally homemade—and

go out trick-or-treating. Halloween is, if you think about it, a ritualized and disguised form of begging by children. Frequently the children are accompanied by their parents, who linger in the background while the neighbors fill up the children's bags with candy. Halloween has roots in medieval celebrations—periods of carnival and license when, briefly, everyday life became festive and unruly. These periods linger in cities and countries where carnival is the time of huge festivities and orgiastic celebrating, as in Rio de Janeiro.

In the San Francisco area, and now throughout the country, many gay adults have started celebrating Halloween. Every year, in San Francisco and other cities, there are huge gay celebrations featuring men and women in all kinds of elaborate costumes.

So Halloween has been turned into a gigantic

TRICK OR TREAT   marketing opportunity—for selling costumes to children and adults, and for selling candy to be given to children who are trick-or-treating. The drugstores and supermarkets are full of huge bags of candy that adults buy and give to children, and racks of Halloween costumes and masks are to be found in stores. Valentine's Day is another huge candy-selling event for merchandisers.

Thanksgiving

Thanksgiving is a national holiday honoring our earliest colonists. According to legend, the colonists held a feast to celebrate their survival, which was largely due to the help of Native Americans. The holiday is celebrated by preparing a large traditional meal, usually featuring a roast turkey and certain other dishes such as sweet potatoes, cranberry sauce, stuffing, and various kinds of pies. This celebration also is one in which grown children often travel considerable distances to dine with their parents, so the airlines and the supermarkets do very well at Thanksgiving.

Generally speaking, the day after Thanksgiving—when we are feeling good because we've eaten well and celebrated together—is the most important shopping day in America. It marks the beginning of the Christmas shopping period, the most important period of consumer consumption in the country.

Christmas

Christmas is the major selling event for merchandisers. Something like 20 percent of all goods and services sold during the year are sold in the Christmas period. This period also accounts for approximately 30 percent of the profits for merchandisers. The Christmas buying period begins in late November, the day after Thanksgiving, and ends on December 24—the day before Christmas. Christmas has now become a period of mandatory gift giving, and the average American family spends hundreds of dollars on Christmas gifts for family and friends.

Gift giving, in one form or another, takes place in many cultures. In the United States and many western European countries, the Christmas period is also one of considerable anxiety. Some people spend more than they should (relative to their finances) and go into debt because of their purchases. There is also the matter of equivalence in gift giving. We want to give people gifts that cost approximately the same amount of money as the gifts we expect to get from them. If we spend too little, we will slight them; and if we spend too much, we will make them feel uncomfortable because they have slighted us.

Due to the stress of the Christmas buying period, many people suffer from anxiety and depression. Ironically, a period devoted (originally, at least) to religious celebration has become highly commercialized, leading many people to argue that we should put the *Christ* back in *Christmas*.

As retailers have found ways to spread consumption throughout the year, the significance of Christmas as an all-important period of consumption has declined. Not so long ago, Christmas represented 25 percent of all purchases made; now it is down to 20 percent.

SUMMARY

In this chapter on the act of consumption, I've considered psychological aspects of consumption, including my notion that one reason we shop is to have our existence acknowledged (by salespeople, and later by the bill in the mail or a line on our credit card bill). I've also considered the tricks we play on ourselves when we purchase things on sale—convincing ourselves that we are spending money and saving money, at the same time. I've dealt with the notion that in consuming products such as soda pop, we are convinced that we are rewarding ourselves with these products, which we richly deserve. I also considered the notion that conspicuous consumption is a sign of success, demonstrated by purchasing so-called status symbols; and that consumption often is not the end point of a narrative, but one that forces us into a chain of secondary purchases.

Next, I dealt with the notion that consumption is connected to mimetic desire and our desire to imitate others. I followed this with a discussion of places where we consume things (department stores, big-box stores, supermarkets) and the language of consumption—how we often use euphemisms to disguise the fact that we have purchased something. Finally, I analyzed the different modes of consumption, the way we purchase things, and the consumer culture calendar, which focuses upon the various holidays that we've turned into sales events and buying opportunities for individuals.

I made considerable use of the ideas of Ernest Dichter, the father of motivation research, who argued that unconscious elements in our psyches are often behind our behavior, including consuming objects and services. When a person clicks a button on an Internet shopping site or reaches for a box of cereal in a supermarket, that action is connected to a myriad of factors. Though we have an enormous amount of information on human motivation and psychology, the act of consumption by a given individual remains something of an enigma.

The field of consumer behavior covers a lot of ground: it is the study of the processes involved when individuals or groups select, purchase, use or dispose of products, services, ideas or experiences to satisfy needs and desires. Consumers take many forms, ranging from a six-year-old child pleading with her mother for wine gums to an executive in a large corporation deciding on an extremely expensive computer system. The items that are consumed can include anything from tinned beans to a massage, democracy, rap music, and even other people (the images of rock stars, for example). Needs and desires to be satisfied range from hunger and thirst to love, status or even spiritual fulfillment. There is a growing interest in consumer behavior, not only in the field of marketing but from the social sciences in general. This follows a growing awareness of the increasing importance of consumption in our daily lives, in our organization of daily activities, in our identity formation, in politics and economic development, and in the flows of global culture, where consumer culture seems to spread, albeit in new forms, from North America and Europe to other parts of the world. Indeed, consumption can be regarded as playing such an important role in our social, psychological, economical, political and cultural lives today that it has become the "vanguard of history." (2002, 5)

—**Michael Solomon, Gary Bamossy, and Soren Askegaard,**
Consumer Behavior: A European Perspective

4

PERSPECTIVES ON CONSUMPTION

In this chapter I deal with anthropological, psychological, and sociological perspectives on consumption. I consider such topics as the nature of myth and what I call the "myth model," which, I suggest, plays an important role in consumer cultures. I focus here on the relation between myth and purchasing a home. I also deal with the way fads and group affiliations affect our behavior as consumers and the way our consumer society has affected the middle classes in the United States.

THE ANTHROPOLOGY OF CONSUMPTION

Many different disciplinary approaches to consumption can be used, for it is a subject that has been of interest to anthropologists, sociologists, psychologists, semioticians, economists, and various other kinds of scholars. Each disciplinary perspective has its strong points but also, due to the limitations of its viewpoint, neglects certain things. I hope that by providing several different ways of looking at consumer societies, I will offer a more comprehensive and balanced view of the matter.

In this analysis, using what I call the myth model, I will deal with purchasing a house—generally the biggest and one of the most important purchasing decisions people make. I will also consider some important mythic aspects to living in a house.

The Nature of Myth

In several other publications, I have developed the myth model. In this model I suggest that many of our acts as individuals—and many of our cultural texts—are based, though we are not aware of it, on some myth. That is, the myth informs many different aspects of our culture, including our everyday-life activities—one of which involves shopping. In one of my seminars several years ago, my students and I took a myth and tried to see how it could be found in historical events, elite culture, popular culture, and everyday life. In short, the implication is that myth has an important role in shaping our behavior, both as individuals and collectively.

I developed this myth model after reading Mircea Eliade's book *The Sacred and the Profane*. In it, the author suggests that many activities in contemporary life can be seen as camouflaged or modernized versions of ancient myths and legends:

> The modern man who feels and claims that he is nonreligious still retains a large stock of camouflaged myths and degenerated rituals. . . . A whole volume could well be written on the myths of modern man, on the mythologies camouflaged in the plays that he enjoys, in the books that he reads. The cinema, that "dream factory," takes over and employs countless mythological motifs—the fight between hero and monster, initiatory combats and ordeals, paradigmatic figures (the maiden, the hero, the paradisal landscape, hell, and so

Our ideas about buying a house in the suburbs may have mythical roots in the Puritans' need to escape from Europe hundreds of years ago.

on). Even reading includes a mythological function, not only because it replaces the recitation of myths in archaic societies and the oral literature that still lives in the rural communities of Europe, but particularly because, through reading, the modern man succeeds in obtaining an "escape from time" comparable to the "emergence from time" effected by myths. (Eliade 1961, 204–5)

For Eliade, *myth* can be understood as the recitation of a sacred history, "a primordial event that took place at the beginning of time" (1961, 95).

Another definition of *myth* can be found in Raphael Patai's *Myth and Modern Man:*

Myth . . . is a traditional religious charter, which operates by validating laws, customs, rites, institutions and beliefs, or explaining sociocultural situations and natural phenomena, and taking the form of stories, believed to be true, about divine beings and heroes. (Patai 1972, 2)

Patai argues that myths play an important role in shaping social life, and that "myth not only validates or authorizes customs, rites, institutions, beliefs, and so forth, but frequently is directly responsible for creating them" (1972, 2).

The Myth of Nature

My analysis, based on Eliade's point about unrecognized myths permeating our culture and Patai's notion that myths help shape institutions and beliefs, suggests there are camouflaged and unrecognized myths that inform many of our texts and many other aspects of our culture, including consumption. The point is that for our purposes, when we read, go shopping, and buy things, we are connecting to ancient myths. Thus, through advertising and other entertainments, we live and shop mythically, even if we may not recognize that such is the case. In this example, I take this myth of nature and show how it informs various aspects of our culture:

Myth/Sacred Story	Adam in the Garden of Eden: theme of natural innocence
Historical Experience	Puritans come to United States to escape corrupt European civilization
Elite Culture	American Adam figure in American novels: *The American,* by Henry James
Popular Culture	Westerns restore natural innocence to virgin land: *Shane,* by Jack Schaefer
Everyday Life	Escape from city and move to suburbs so kids can play on grass

As this model suggests, there are hidden sacred or mythic roots to many different aspects of our lives. In the United States, where nature is an important part of our cultural imagination—probably the most important element in it—manifestations of the biblical story of Adam and Eve, living in paradise in a state of nature, can be found in everything. It is evident in our historical experience—leaving "corrupt" Europe to establish a new "innocent" society in the great American wilderness—and in our elite literature, with its Adamic figures in many novels, as well as in our westerns and science fiction stories.

Our popular culture texts, such as Westerns, often deal with getting rid of evildoers and villains of one sort or another, so that—in theory at least—a more paradisical society can be reestablished in nature. In the seminar I mentioned earlier, when we had run through the Adamic myth and shown how it was connected to our ideas about nature, one of my students, a woman with two children, slapped her head and said, "So that's why I bought a house in the suburbs." Buying a house in the suburbs is similar in nature, let me suggest, to escaping from Europe and all that it stood for in the minds of the Puritans.

The Mythical Importance of Houses

Eliade also deals with the psychological and mythical importance of houses in his book. He writes:

To us, it seems an inescapable conclusion that *the religious man sought to live as near as possible to the Center of the World.* He knew that his country lay at the midpoint of the earth; he knew too that his city constituted the navel of the universe, and, above all, that the temple or the palace were veritably Centers of the World. But he also wanted his own house to be the Center . . . and, in fact, as we shall see, houses are held to be at the Center of the World and, on the microscopic scale, to reproduce the universe. (Eliade 1961, 43)

This matter of being in the center is, of course, existential; each person sees his home as at the center of the world—and it is, for most people. In modern times, our attitudes about our houses have become desacralized. But they still retain a residue of the sacred that we can feel, even if we can't articulate how we feel. "Everyone's house is his castle," we sometimes say, not recognizing that, psychologically speaking, it is also his church.

I happen to come from Boston, which describes itself, modestly, as "the Hub of the Universe." This description ties into Eliade's notions about our desire to live in the center of the world. Furnishing a house is analogous, in the sacred perspective on things that he argues, to creating the world.

THE PSYCHOLOGY OF CONSUMPTION

I have already dealt with some psychological matters related to consumption, especially in my use of the ideas of Ernest Dichter (2002), but there are other psychological factors to be considered. I start with a discussion of two kinds of shopping personalities or types of shoppers—maximizers and satisfizers.

Maximizers versus Satisfizers

Psychologist Barry Schwartz has written a book, *The Paradox of Choice,* in which he offers some interesting insights into consumer behavior. In an article he wrote based on his book, "When It's All Too Much," Schwartz describes what happened when he went to a store to buy a pair of jeans:

One day I went to the Gap to buy a pair of jeans. A salesperson asked if she could help. "I want a pair of jeans—32-28," I said. "Do you want them slim fit, easy fit, relaxed fit, baggy or extra baggy?" she replied. "Do you want them stone-washed, acid-washed, or distressed? Do you want them button-fly or zipper-fly? Do you want them faded or regular?" (Schwartz 2004, 4)

Schwartz observes that purchasing jeans used to be a five-minute operation but now can take a long time because it is such a complex decision.
There are now, he also points out, eighty types of painkillers and forty
kinds of toothpaste. Ironically, he suggests, drawing on the work of other
psychologists, "Increased choice and increased affluence have, in fact,
been accompanied by decreased well-being" (Schwartz 2004, 4). He cites
figures showing that more people are depressed now and suggests that "as
we become freer to pursue and do whatever we want, we get less and less
happy," in part because of increased expectations we have about every aspect of our lives.

This notion is reflected in two diametrically opposed kinds of shoppers—
what Schwartz calls *maximizers* and *satisfizers*. (This material comes, in part,
from an interview he had on the *Lehrer News Hour*, December 26, 2004.)

Maximizers	Satisfizers
Must have very best	Good enough is OK
High expectations	Low expectations
Anxiety	Ease

The problem that maximizers face is that in always searching for the best
product and the best deal, they become highly stressed and anxiety ridden.
Any choice you make, Schwartz points out, involves ruling out other
choices. The important thing, he suggests, is to accept what is "good
enough" and not agonize over missing out on what might possibly be a better deal.

His advice, that we should moderate our expectations, is very sound.
Maximizers can never be satisfied, because no matter what kind of a deal
they've made on some purchase, in principle there always could be a better
one. It's important for one's psychological health, Schwartz suggests, to
moderate one's expectations and recognize the virtue of the satisfizers' perspective on things. He suggests that we have too many choices.

The question arises, then: Why are there so many different kinds of jeans
and toothpaste and painkillers? Could it be connected, somehow, to the different kinds of consumers that marketers have elaborated in their various
schemes? If we have sixty-six different kinds of consumer types, as Claritas
suggests, there's reason to understand why we have so many different kinds
of everything.

Schwartz's theory about maximizers and satisfizers helps explain the behavior of those mythical donkeys that find themselves sitting between two

piles of hay. Some philosophers have suggested that a donkey placed equidistant between two piles of hay would starve to death because it couldn't decide which pile of hay was closer. If the donkey were a maximizer, it probably would starve to death; it would be paralyzed, unable to decide which of the two piles of hay was closer, and thus a "better deal" in that it required less expenditure of effort to get the hay. But donkeys are satisfizers. If placed equidistant between two piles of hay, they would eat one pile of hay; and then, if they were still hungry, they would eat the other pile of hay—not worrying about whether they'd walked farther to get to one pile of hay than the other.

Id, Ego, and Superego

I have already dealt with Freud's *topographic model* of the human psyche, which divides it into an unconscious level (a level we cannot access, though it shapes much of our behavior), a preconscious level, and a conscious level. We can also understand consumption by using Freud's *structural model* of the psyche, which suggests that there is an endless conflict between the id ("I want it now") elements of our psyches and the superego ("You can't afford it, and you'll be sorry if you buy it") elements of our psyches. Mediating between these two forces is the ego, which attempts to keep both id and superego balanced by arguing ("Why don't you think about it more" and "You really can't afford this, but maybe you can afford that").

Advertising agencies and companies involved in consumer products appeal to the id elements in people, seeking to generate an emotional appeal that leads individuals to overcome the strictures of their superegos and purchase things because they get pleasure (or anticipate pleasure) from doing so. This relationship is shown in the following chart:

Id	Ego	Superego
Emotion	Rationality	Conscience
Buy	Think	Don't buy
Want	Afford	Need

Some consumption is based on rationality and need. For example, an appliance breaks down and has to be replaced. But a great deal is based on desire rather than need, on momentary passions rather than logical thinking.

The Pavlovian Perspective

For those who prefer a behaviorist orientation to advertising rather than a Freudian one, a *Wall Street Journal* article from several years ago is of considerable interest ("Coca-Cola Turns to Pavlov . . .," January 19, 1984, 34). In this article, the author suggests that Russian psychologist Ivan Pavlov, not Freud, should be considered the real founder of modern advertising techniques. Pavlov found he could make dogs salivate by ringing a bell whenever they were given food. The dogs became "conditioned" by the bell and would salivate whenever they heard the bell.

The article explains how some advertising executives at Coca-Cola were arguing that people respond to commercials the way dogs used to respond to Pavlov's bell. The dogs learned to associate food with the ringing of the bell, which gave the bell a new meaning. In the same way, Coca-Cola advertising executives believed they could make commercials that "conditioned" people exposed to these commercials to want to drink Coca-Cola. Joel S. Dubrow, a communications research manager at Coca-Cola, was quoted in the article as saying he thought that Pavlov should be considered the father of modern advertising. As Dubrow explained, "Pavlov took a neutral object and, by associating it with a meaningful object, made it a symbol of something else; he imbued it with imagery, he gave it added value." And that, Dubrow suggested, was what Coke was trying to do with its advertising.

This perspective on consumption, which reduces people to conditioned responders to stimuli, is, I would argue, terribly dehumanizing and probably simplistic. But what if Coca-Cola is right?

Whether consumers buy things because of hidden imperatives in the unconscious elements in their psyches, the domination of id elements in their psyches, or because they are responding (like dogs, or, in more modern cases, laboratory rats) to certain stimuli that condition them, the picture isn't pretty. Further, the notion of human autonomy as regards the matter of buying things, and perhaps regarding anything else, becomes increasingly questionable.

Neuromarketing

Thanks to magnetic resonance imaging (MRI), we now know more about what goes on in the minds of consumers as they purchase various products. In his article "A Probe inside the Mind of the Shopper," Jerome Burne explains that a new technique of interpreting brain activity during purchasing times, called neuromarketing, can help marketing managers find out how consumers make their decisions. He writes that neuromarketing can "provide snapshot images of brain activity in crucial moments of retail choice. Scientists have been putting volunteers into MRI . . . scanners to find out what goes on in their brains when they look at pictures of consumer goods" (*Financial Times,* November 27, 2003, 13).

These scanners, Burne writes, were used in trying to figure out a conundrum in cola marketing—explaining why Coca-Cola outsells Pepsi when blind tasting generally shows that people prefer the taste of Pepsi. He explains that as soon as people find out they are drinking Coca-Cola, they change their opinions, demonstrating that brand images play an important role in consumer preferences. In his research, Burne studied the role of the ventral putamen in the brain. He concluded that consumers were affected by their memories as well as by other impressions of Coca-Cola; that is, their thinking was shaped by Coca-Cola's brand image. A strong brand image, he concluded, can override a person's taste buds.

Burne suggests that the development of neuromarketing may lead to its taking the place of focus groups, with this methodology being applied to politicians as well as colas and other consumer products. He adds that other techniques, such as using electroencephalograms (EEGs), are being used to determine how well people remember commercial messages to which they are exposed. Whether neurological techniques will lead to a new means of doing marketing research remains to be seen, because neurologists still don't know enough about how the brain works to be certain of the significance of the results they obtain using MRIs and EEGs.

Collectors

Here I discuss another aspect of consuming—people who are collectors. They become interested in some object, whether it is cars or postage stamps or statues of elephants or a certain kind of glassware, and collect huge numbers of these objects. Collectors tend to have certain traits.

First, collectors strive for a kind of totalism or completion, obtaining as many objects as they can of whatever it is they collect. They select one kind of object that, for one reason or another, interests them; and they aim to get as many choice examples of this item as they can. By narrowing their range, they can achieve a kind of domination. This is a form of mastery, which manifests itself in purchasing objects of their desire. The objects are purchased for the psychological gratifications they confer on the collector, though there may be commercial aspects of collecting. In many cases, collectors compete for a given object, thus giving collecting an element of game playing and forcing collectors to try to outmaneuver one another.

Collectors can show connoisseurship and manifest their expertise in the choices they make. Collectors, as a rule, want only choice items; obtaining the best items involves, generally speaking, a certain amount of study and learning about the objects being collected. Thus, collecting may involve learning a great deal about history and other matters relating to the objects being collected. There are, of course, some collectors who aren't interested in being selective and collect as many objects as they can. For them, quantity counts.

CONSUMER CULTURE FACTOID

Often regarded as lonely if not pathological eccentrics, collectors actually express a powerful communal drive in a solitary age. United by the universal language of e-mail and eBay and a vast constellation of shows, societies and publications that bring them together, collectors create a deepening pattern in the carpet of contemporary life. While the urge to acquire first-edition books, Japanese woodblock prints, baseball cards, Beanie Babies or vintage Bartolos might be seen as a telling reflection of consumerist excess and licensed dysfunction, it is also a way of apprehending a bewildering world and finding one's place in it.

Acknowledging aspects of compulsion and raw competition, UCSF clinical professor of psychiatry Graeme Hanson sees collectors as a blend of acquisitiveness, intellectual curiosity, a desire to possess and organize tangible objects, the lure of immortality and "a certain amount of showing off."

Steven Winn, "Call Them What You Will—Obsessive Compulsive, Eccentrics, Materialist Philosophers or Pack-Rat Artists— Collectors' 'Unruly Passions' Make Sense of Our World." *San Francisco Chronicle*, December 15, 2003, p. D-1.

Collectors, we must realize, are a kind of consumer. But this element tends to be hidden by the other elements of collecting, which distract our attention from the fact that being a collector involves buying things. Thus, collectors get some gratifications from their behavior: the pleasure of buying things without any of the negative aspects involved in being a consumer; a kind of pride of ownership; and the development of an area of expertise, related to the objects that are collected.

There is an element of obsessive-compulsive behavior in collectors. They can, in some cases, become emotionally involved or overly preoccupied with obtaining the objects they desire. And their compulsive behavior can affect their lives in profound ways—determining, for example, where they travel and what they do when they travel.

The Marketing Personality

One consequence of living in a consumer society, where marketing plays such an important role in the scheme of things, is that many people develop what might be described as a marketing personality. By this I mean they learn to "sell" or market themselves to others by creating a personality geared toward finding acceptance among whatever individuals or groups with which they are involved. People with a marketing personality spend their lives "selling" themselves to others. This means they change their personalities to fit the needs of the day, and they fail to develop a coherent sense of themselves. (The term *personality* comes from the Latin term *persona*, or "mask.")

Due to this kind of behavior, people become alienated from themselves, estranged from what we might call their "true selves." As Fritz Pappenheim explains in his book *The Alienation of Modern Man:*

> There seems to be a tendency in all of us to become indifferent bystanders. In the way we associate with other people or respond to important happenings we tend toward a fragmentary encounter. We do not relate to the other person as a whole or to the event as a whole, but we isolate the one part which is important to us and remain more or less remote observers of the rest.
>
> The person who thus splits the real into two parts becomes divided in his own self. . . . There is something uncanny in the condition of man when he becomes a stranger to himself; but it is a fate which shapes the lives of many of us. We seem to be caught in a frightening contradiction. In order to assert ourselves as individuals, we relate only to those phases of reality which seem to promote the attainment of our objectives and we remain divorced from the rest of it. (Pappenheim 1967, 12–13)

Thus, when we develop a personality based on marketing ourselves to others, we become separated from our true selves—a separation that we may not recognize intellectually but which we feel, especially when we face difficulties. This marketing personality may be tied to our postmodern societies, in which changes of identity—or of appearances, at least—are the norm.

Pappenheim's point is that when we focus our attention on calculating how to market ourselves to others instead of developing a coherent character and self, we become alienated from ourselves and ultimately suffer from this alienation. We've made a sale, to so speak; but at the cost of losing our identities, our sense of self. Pappenheim's discussion of Arthur Miller's *Death of a Salesman* deals with this matter:

> Many individuals have found their own lives portrayed in Arthur Miller's *Death of a Salesman*. It shows Willy Loman—the "other-directed man" personified—striving all his life to be popular and "liked" but remaining absolutely lonesome and irrelevant, forever dreaming that "personality always wins the day" but in reality destined, as his wife fears, "to fall into his grave like an old dog." (Pappenheim 1967, 34)

For decades, this play has had the ability to stir powerful emotions in the audiences who watch it, which suggests that it connects with anxieties that many people have about their own lives. The fate of Willy Loman, the ultimate personification of the marketing personality, resonates with all of us.

Find a Husband after 35

Rachel Greenwald, a marketer who studied at the Harvard Business School, has written a book, *Find a Husband after 35*, that teaches women how to "market" themselves. In an article titled "35+ and Single? Put on a Push-Up Bra and Market Yourself, Author Says," Greenwald explains that while coaching a single 41-year-old friend, she had an epiphany:

> I realized I was telling her classic business approaches to her dating life. . . . As we talked about improving her appearance, we were talking about packaging. (*Jewish Bulletin of Northern California*, October 3, 2004, 8)

Greenwald has a fifteen-step action program that teaches women how to market themselves and find a husband. She also has a website (www .findahusbandafter35.com) that offers other help and support groups.

It might seem crass to say so, but finding a husband does involve marketing oneself—dressing well, looking attractive, being attentive, developing a pleasing personality—though we tend to push those aspects of the dating game into our unconscious as we search for a husband or wife. In a marketing society, everything is eventually reduced to selling, in the final analysis.

This rational approach to dating shouldn't be difficult for women and men who have already developed a certain expertise in marketing themselves when dealing with another important matter—selling themselves to college admissions officers at selective universities. They sell themselves by creating a résumé full of the activities admissions officers are supposedly searching for: community work, membership in various school clubs, and that kind of thing. I know of one person who suggested to his son that he learn to play the bassoon so he might better his chances of getting into Harvard, which needed good musicians for its student orchestra and would probably be looking for good bassoonists. The son, I should add, got into Harvard.

THE SOCIOLOGY OF CONSUMPTION

I've already considered one sociological perspective on consumption in my discussion of the grid-group theory of Mary Douglas, a social anthropologist (see chapter 1). Her argument, let us recall, is that in modern societies there are four consumer cultures or lifestyles (elitist, individualist, egalitarian, and fatalist) and that it is membership in one of these consumer cultures—that is, group affiliation—rather than psychological factors that shapes people's consumer choices. Douglas can be seen as a kind of bridge between psychological and sociological theories of consumption.

Sociologists focus their attention on groups and institutions, so a sociological approach to consumer cultures would be concerned with collective behavior and phenomena related to consumption, such as fads, product crazes, functional considerations, uses and gratifications, social class, and other group-related matters connected to consumer behavior. I begin with a discussion of Cabbage Patch Kids, which were a big fad in 1983.

Fads, Crazes, and Other Forms of Consumer Madness

Twenty years ago there was a craze for Cabbage Patch dolls—ugly little dolls that, somehow, struck a receptive chord in children and became a must-have toy. In a *Newsweek* article on the subject, "Oh, You Beautiful Dolls!" (subtitled "They're Rioting in the Malls for the Chance to Cuddle with Cabbage Patch Kids"), we read:

> It was as if an army had been turned loose on the nation's shopping malls, braving the *Ficus* trees, sloshing through the fountains, searching for the legendary stockrooms said to be filled with thousands of the dough-face, chinless, engagingly homely dolls that have become the Holy Grail of the 1983 Christmas shopping season: the Cabbage Patch Kids. Clerks were helpless before the onslaught.

Newspapers at the time were filled with stories about desperate parents searching all over for the dolls. What happened with the Cabbage Patch Kids has occurred routinely over the years as this or that toy becomes "hot" and everyone wants one. A month or two later, as with every other toy, children became interested in something else.

We see faddish behavior in all the different diet programs that have been popular over the years. As I write this, the Atkins diet has become a real craze; even McDonald's is offering products for those interested in reducing or eliminating, as much as possible, their intake of carbohydrates. The Atkins diet has also led to a large number of businesses catering to people interested in following the diet, and it has had a powerful impact on the meat industry.

Ironically, just as the Atkins diet was becoming a major fad, the death of a single "mad" cow generated a nationwide wave of fear and anxiety about eating meat, so diet-conscious consumers in the United States (and the other countries that import our beef) find themselves on the horns of a dilemma: They want to eat meat to follow the Atkins diet, but if they do, they may be at risk (even if it is very small) of getting a horrible disease.

The Crowd and Consumer Behavior

To understand why fads occur, it is useful to examine the ideas of the great sociologist Gustave Le Bon, author of the classic work *The Crowd*. He explains that people, even though isolated from one another, "may acquire at certain moments, and under the influence of certain violent emotions—such, for example, as a great national event—the characteristics of a psychological crowd" (Le Bon 1960, 24). As Le Bon explains:

The most striking peculiarity presented by a psychological crowd is the following: Whoever be the individuals that compose it, however like or unlike be their mode of life, their occupations, their character, or their intelligence, the fact that they have been transformed into a crowd puts them in possession of a sort of collective mind which makes them feel, think, and act in a manner quite different from that in which each individual of them would feel, think, and act were he in a state of isolation. (Le Bon 1960)

So becoming a member of a psychological crowd—now facilitated greatly by ubiquitous mass media and advertising—makes us act in ways that we would not ordinarily act as individuals. As far as consumption is concerned, such crowds become susceptible to various fads and crazes. Le Bon is very much aware of the power of drama, arguing that images found in theatrical representations have enormous power over people:

Nothing has a greater effect on the imagination of crowds of every category than theatrical representations. The entire audience experiences at the same time the same emotions, and if these emotions are not at once transformed into acts, it is because the most unconscious spectator cannot ignore that he is the victim of illusions, and that he has laughed or wept over imaginary adventures. Sometimes, however, the sentiments suggested by the images are so strong that they tend, like habitual suggestions, to transform themselves into acts. (Le Bon 1960, 88)

Advertisements are, we must realize, the preeminent form of what Le Bon would call "theatrical representations." The act that advertisers hope for is a decision, after seeing one commercial or a hundred commercials, by consumers to buy the products or services the advertisers are pitching. It's always interesting to switch off the sound when watching commercials and focus on the extremely expressive facial expressions and body language of the actors in these minidramas. But we are also exposed to thousands of print advertisements in our newspapers and magazines, so we live in societies permeated with advertising.

We Are Where We Shop

A sociology professor from Brooklyn College, Sharon Zukin, has written a book titled *Point of Purchase: How Shopping Changes American Culture.* In a *New York Times* op-ed article (November 28, 2003), "We Are Where We Shop," Zukin argues that in the past century the United States has transformed itself into a shopping nation. She contends that the low prices we pay for food and other products (relative to most other countries) represent "a Faustian deal with the culture of shopping" because the social costs of maintaining this culture are very high.

The middle classes, Zukin suggests, have maintained their status by paying low prices for consumer goods—and, until recent years, housing. We have an illusion that because all classes now shop in the same stores, we are an egalitarian society in which everyone is searching for good deals in what Zukin calls our "bargain culture." This represents a strange version of democracy—equal access to bargains in strip malls and gigantic box stores. Instead of paying people more, the author suggests, we have made goods less expensive. But now, as the economy has faltered in recent years, many people are finding it increasingly difficult to pay their bills.

The title of Zukin's article suggests something else: For many people, their sense of themselves—their social identity—is shaped in considerable measure by the kinds of stores they go to and the kinds of things they can afford.

Upscale and Downscale, Entry-Level and Top-of-the-Line

In modern societies, we've developed elaborate ways of categorizing stores and the goods they sell. If we have sixty-six distinctive consumer clus-

CONSUMER CULTURE FACTOID

When General Motors began gearing up new advertising for its GMC line, marketers prowled for ideas to help give the brand a unique theme. They quickly found one. Consumers saw GMC as the pickup of choice for professional tradesmen. Some even believed GMCs were engineered to tougher specifications than Chevy trucks, even though they were virtually identical in design. GM realized it had tapped a potentially powerful marketing tool: professional-grade products. "They were about capabilities, a certain way of feeling and confidence," says Pontiac/GMC chief Lynn Myers. "We decided to capture that gestalt."

Leslie Smith Jr., "If the Pros Use a Tool or a Toothbrush, It Will Sell," *USA Today*, December 17, 2003, p. 1.

ters in the United States, as the Claritas typology suggests, then obviously lots of consumers make all kinds of distinctions between different products. We use the term *upscale* to describe products that appeal to affluent consumers, who find these products at expensive department stores like Neiman-Marcus and certain expensive boutiques. The term *downscale* describes less expensive or inexpensive products found at stores like Target and Wal-Mart.

The matter is further complicated because we distinguish between "entry-level" products and "top-of-the-line" products. Thus, when it comes to cars, certain BMWs are seen as entry level while other BMWs are seen as top of the line. The entry-level BMWs often cost half as much as the top-of-the-line BMWs. So, while a BMW may be an upscale automobile, an entry-level BMW doesn't have the cachet that a top-of-the-line BMW has.

You can see that when it comes to judging and placing consumer goods, there are many different factors to keep in mind. When it comes to buying cars, each consumer has to decide whether it is better to have a top-of-the-line cheaper brand or an entry-level expensive brand. For people who are not concerned with prestige and showing that they are successful, all these calculations are pointless. But many other people believe that the car you drive is who you are.

SUMMARY

In this chapter, I have considered the act of consumption from three perspectives: anthropology, psychology, and sociology.

In "The Anthropology of Consumption," I dealt with the nature of myth and suggested that many of our activities can be seen as modernized and camouflaged versions of ancient myths. We are unaware of these myths, though we may dimly perceive that there are connections between our celebrations of certain holidays (New Year's Eve parties) and ancient myths. I used mythic attitudes toward nature, which play an important role in the American consciousness, as an example of how myths can inform and are reflected in various aspects of our culture, including that of buying a house in the suburbs.

In "The Psychology of Consumption," I dealt with a number of factors that relate to consumption and the human psyche. I discussed the ideas of Barry Schwartz, a psychologist who investigated the problems people face when dealing with choice. Schwartz suggested that there are two diametrically opposed types of consumers: maximizers (seeking the perfect deal) and satisfizers (who seek things that are good enough).

I then explained how Freud's id, ego, superego thesis about the human psyche could be applied to consumption. I contrasted that theory with the Pavlovian approach, which suggests that much of our behavior is conditioned, and noted that we aren't too far removed from Pavlov's celebrated dogs that learned to salivate when a bell was rung. This led to a discussion of collectors, who can be described (at their most extreme) as obsessive-compulsives, who have channeled their behavior into consuming certain objects of interest to them. I then discussed the new technique of neuromarketing, which uses neurological techniques to understand better how the brain works when people are involved in consuming products.

I concluded my discussion with a suggestion that in societies in which marketing is all-important, people develop what might be described as "marketing personalities" and become so involved with marketing themselves that they lose any sense of who they really are. As an example of this, I cited Rachel Greenwald's book telling women over age 35 how to market themselves in order to find a husband.

In "The Sociology of Consumption," I discussed the sociological approach to consumer cultures, dealing with some of the more interesting aspects of consumer behavior. I then considered the matter of fads and crazes, which erupt from time to time and lead to frenzied behavior on the part of people caught up in these fads. I used Gustave Le Bon's work on crowds, in his classic book *The Crowd,* to deal with the theoretical underpinnings of this kind of behavior. And I dealt not only with the importance—to people's identities and sense of self—of where people shop, but with the complications involved in pigeonholing products: determining whether an upscale, entry-level car is better than a top-of-the-line, more downscale one. Consumers who care about prestige and "face" have to take many different matters into consideration.

The study of media genres from the semiotic perspective was initiated . . . by Roland Barthes in the 1950s. Barthes applied basic sign theory . . . to the analysis of all kinds of media spectacles and genres, showing how it can expose the implicit meanings built into them. Recall that a sign is defined as something physical (X) standing for something else (Y), material or conceptual, in some particular way (X = Y). The sign can be a simple form such as a word, or a complex form such as a novel or radio programme. The latter is designated a *text* in semiotic theory. But a text is still a sign. That is why, for instance, we read and remember a novel as a singular form (X), not as an aggregate of its individual words, having a specific type of meaning or range of meanings (Y), that we derive from it on the basis of personal, social, and other kinds of experiences.

Barthes' goal was to expose pop culture as a huge distraction factory, aimed at uprooting the traditional forms of art and meaning-making. In so doing, he showed that it constitutes an overarching system of signs that recycles deeply-embedded meanings with Western culture, subverting them to commercial ends. (2002, 23)

—Marcel Danesi, *Understanding Media Semiotics*

⑤

THE SEMIOTICS OF SHOPPING

Semiotics is the science of signs (from *seméion,* the Greek term for "sign"), and it is concerned with how people find meaning in things. A sign is anything that represents or can be used to stand for something else. The signs that concern us in this book are those involved with consumption and, more particularly, with matters such as signs of lifestyle, taste, and socioeconomic class found in objects and texts, among other things. Words, facial expressions, body language, design, spatiality, color, texture, typefaces, music, sound effects—all of these are signs that people have to learn to "read" or interpret to understand print advertisements, commercials, the significance of various products, and texts (works of imagination) of all kinds.

We are all, it could be said, amateur semioticians, even though we may not be aware of the concepts underlying this science. We all practice "reading" people in real life and in texts such as plays, movies, novels, television shows, advertisements, and commercials. I will now discuss two seminal books that use semiotic theory to investigate consumer cultures—one in the United States and the other in France.

The semiotic approach can be applied to a variety of consumer products, including detergent and plastics.

THE MECHANICAL BRIDE

In his book, *The Mechanical Bride: Folklore of Industrial Man*, Marshall McLuhan offered many semiotic analyses of American commercial culture, though he didn't use semiotic terms. This book, published in 1951, was one of the earliest examinations of what we now call consumer culture. In his essay "The Mechanical Bride," McLuhan considers the way some women use their bodies:

> To the mind of the modern girl, legs, like busts, are power points which she has been taught to tailor, but as parts of the success kit rather than erotically or sensuously. She swings her legs from the hip with masculine drive and confidence. She knows that "a long-legged gal can go places." As such, her legs are not intimately associated with her taste or her unique self but are merely display objects like the grill work on a car. They are date-baited power levers for the management of the male audience. (1951, 98)

Later in the essay McLuhan deals with the relationship between sex and technology and the notion that the human body should be seen as a kind of love machine "capable merely of specific thrills." Sex now, he asserts, is reduced to a problem in mechanics and hygiene.

In his book, McLuhan analyzes comic strips, advertisements, the front page of newspapers, and so forth to determine the values behind them. His method, as he explains in his preface, is "to apply the method of art analysis to the critical evaluation of society. . . . Art criticism is free to point to the various means employed to get the effect" (McLuhan 1951, vi). What McLuhan calls "art criticism" is, in actuality, semiotic analysis—an investigation of the signs, and what they reveal about American society, evident in the consumer culture in which McLuhan found himself.

MYTHOLOGIES

If semiotic analysis of consumer cultures was implicit in McLuhan's *Mechanical Bride,* it was explicit in Roland Barthes' *Mythologies.* Barthes has written on literary theory, semiotic theory, literature, and many other subjects; but it is his *Mythologies* that is of most importance for our concerns. In this book he deals with such topics as margarine, soap powders and detergents, toys, wine and milk, plastic, and a new Citroen car, among other things. As Barthes explains in the preface to the 1972 edition of his book:

> This book has a double theoretical framework: on the one hand, an ideological critique bearing on the language of so-called mass-culture; on the other, a first attempt to analyze semiologically the mechanics of this language. I had just read Saussure and as a result acquired the conviction that by treating "collective representations" as sign-systems, one might hope to go further than the pious show of unmasking them and account *in detail* for the mystification which transforms petit-bourgeois culture into a universal nature. (Barthes 1972, 9)

Barthes applied his semiological (now we use the term *semiotics* instead) approach, then, to various commonplace aspects of French culture to understand the role they played in its mystification.

In his chapter "Soap-Powders and Detergents" he deals, among other things, with the difference between the two. In the following list are the differences that Barthes considers:

Soap Powders	Detergents
Persil	Omo
Separating agents	Mode of action
Liberates objects from dirt	Consumer accomplice in liberation
Keeps public order	Foam as luxury

He explains:

> "*Persil* Whiteness" for instance, bases its prestige on the evidence of a result; it calls into play vanity, a social concern with appearances, by offering for comparison two objects, one of which is *whiter* than the other. Advertisements for *Omo* also indicate the effect of the product (and in a superlative fashion, incidentally), but they chiefly reveal a mode of action; in doing so, they involve the consumer in a kind of direct experience of the substance, make him the accomplice of a liberation rather than the beneficiary of a result; matter here is endowed with value-bearing states. (Barthes 1972, 57)

Omo, he adds, takes advantage of two of these states, "the deep" and "the foamy." If we say that Omo cleans deep, that means that linen, which it is often used to clean, is deep; and if Omo generates lots of foam, it signifies luxury (a semiotic convention equates foam and luxury) and something mysterious as well—the capacity to make something (foam) out of nothing. These two products, oppositional in relation to their means of cleaning, are unified, however, Barthes points out, at one level: They are both made by the Dutch company Unilever.

The semiotic approach looks at consumer culture in view of its most interesting and important signs. These signs are found in advertisements, in the designs of products, and in the way these products are given a role in our lives. A useful metaphor for understanding consumption, as I pointed out earlier, is to see it as a kind of theater in which consumers are the lead actors and actresses, and the various stores in which they buy things are similar to the sets found in a play—each set is designed to convey certain ideas and feelings in spectators.

STORES AS SETTINGS FOR CONSUMPTION

If we adopt a theatrical metaphor for shopping, we see different kinds of stores as generating certain moods and feelings in spectators and actors. In the following chart I suggest some of the main kinds of stores and say something about their design and the feelings their designs are meant to generate.

Kind of Store	Size	Look	Claim to Fame
Boutiques	Small	Arty	Original products
Supermarkets	Medium	Orderly	Functionality
Department stores	Large	Elegant	Abundance
Big-box stores	Very large	Industrial	Cheap prices

Thus boutiques and boutique-like stores, which are generally small and arty, suggest intimacy, specialization, unusual and original products, and personal attention. In boutiques for clothes, for example, you often find clothes not available elsewhere. Clerks at these stores often are very stylish and generally are quite attractive. In boutique-like specialty stores for coffee and tea, for example, you find unusual blends and high-grade products.

Supermarkets are, as a rule, medium-sized stores whose look is very organized. Their claim to fame is that they are very functional—in essence, they're machines for making foods and other products (they often carry 30,000 different products) easily available. Supermarkets are also at war with fast-food restaurants for lunchtime dollars and with pharmacies for selling prescriptions. Many supermarkets have banks in them, as well as coffee shops. These stores are designed to make people linger, moving away from the perimeter and deeper into the store for products like dog and cat food and cereals. Research shows that the longer people remain in supermarkets, the more they spend. This is because many patrons buy things on impulse and don't stick to a shopping list.

Department stores are large and use their spaciousness to generate feelings of well-being and plenitude. They use lighting, music, space, and color to create the effects they want—a kind of luxuriousness, but one that is accessible to the ordinary person. Upscale department stores such as Nordstrom, for example, have pianists playing to suggest refinement and class. Many department stores have different looks in different areas—catering, for example, to teenagers and young people in areas with loud music and images of rock stars and celebrities.

Big-box stores, such as Costco, use the industrial aesthetic to suggest that they are all business and that they are eliminating frills so as to give their customers the best prices possible. These stores, generally large warehouse-like buildings, have few clerks; shoppers are left on their own. On the other hand, you need to be a member to be able to shop in these stores, so they combine exclusivity with a kind of no-nonsense approach to shopping. Shoppers in these stores are members of a club, so to speak, that is dedicated to shopping.

OLD TOWNS

We see the importance of consumer aesthetics in what are called "old towns"—in many cities, these are areas from the twenties and thirties that somehow escaped being bulldozed and retain their original look. They are characterized by an aesthetic from the early years of the twentieth century, which means that the stores (and the kinds of stores), their windows, their signs, their furniture, and their spatiality reflect the period when they were built.

These areas were once considered to be blighted and ugly. In recent years, however, developers have realized that these old towns have a kind of charm and appeal to shoppers, in reaction to the sterility of some malls; and so these areas have been fixed up to create in our imaginations an illusion of old-fashioned Main Streets.

People who go to old towns are able to experience the pleasure of a cultural regression, to a time when life—so we imagine—was simpler and

"Old towns" attempt to re-create old-fashioned Main Streets that appeal to the consumer's sense of nostalgia.

times were better. My wife and I recently visited one old-town area, where we came across a drugstore with a soda fountain like the ones we were familiar with when we were young. We went in and ordered ice-cream floats—yet another regression, as the psychologists would put it, in the service of our egos. Eating ice cream, which means so much to us when we are children, enables us to regress—if only for a moment—to our earlier years, when we were young and innocent. We didn't know that ice cream was "bad" for us, with its high fat content and calories.

The look of these old towns has been copied in some malls, which attempt to piggyback on the warm feelings people get from visiting old towns; but the synthetic old towns in malls, as a rule, don't generate the same emotions in people. An old town, from the theatrical perspective I dealt with earlier, becomes a setting for us to perform our roles as consumers in a different ambiance—one of innocence, authenticity, and simplicity. Disneyland also has a synthetic Main Street that is, it could be argued, an approximation or simulation of real Main Streets as they existed in earlier years and as they exist now in our cultural imagination.

SIGNIFIERS OF LUXURY ON CRUISES

Cruises have become increasingly popular in recent years; they are one of the fastest-growing segments of the travel industry. The cruise lines have had to fight an image in most people's minds that cruises are luxuries designed mainly for rich, elderly people. Many cruises actually are quite inexpensive. And young and middle-aged people frequently take cruises because they offer a considerable amount of value for the money.

It may seem to be an oxymoron, but cruise lines tend to sell their cruises as "affordable luxuries." The cruise liners are themselves quite beautiful, and there's something fascinating about being on a ship. Cruises are "luxurious" in that the ships are generally elegantly appointed, often with original paintings on the stairwells, beautiful teak decks, elaborate "gourmet" lunches and dinners (often six or seven courses), tea services in the afternoons, concerts and lots of music all the time, and free room service. (For many people, room service is very appealing—a signifier, in the popular mind, of luxurious living.) But many cruises, especially in the off-seasons, are relatively inexpensive, costing as little as $45 or $50 a night per person on "premium" lines such as Holland American, Princess, and Celebrity.

For example, a brochure I got (*Ship 'n' Shore Cruise Connoisseurs,* January–February 2004) from Celebrity Lines advertises a 15-day, 14-night cruise in the western Caribbean on its ship the *Zenith* for $599 for an inside cabin, including the port charge. That's approximately $42 a night, though one must add $10 a day (total) per person for tips for the waiter, assistant waiter, and room steward. That comes to $52 a day, for which you get fourteen nights on the ship, travel to a number of islands, very fine meals, excellent entertainment every evening, and many other things. The *Zenith* cruise is an unusual bargain, but many bargains can be had for people who wish to take cruises.

It is possible, of course, to spend $300 a person per night on some ultra-luxury lines, such as Radisson Seven Seas (8 days/7 nights Caribbean, $2,208), Seabourn, and Crystal. In relation to the semiotics of luxury, however, most ships now closely approximate many of the features in the ultra-luxury lines, for a great deal less money. So cruise lines provide, we might say, luxury for the masses. They are able to serve elaborate meals because of economies of scale—they buy enormous quantities of food and get very favorable prices—and because they exploit, to varying degrees, the third world people who work on the ships.

SUMMARY

In this chapter I used semiotics to deal with consumer cultures based on their use of signifiers, of one sort or another, to sell people products and services. I considered the work of Marshall McLuhan, whose book *The Mechanical Bride* can be considered one of the earliest semiotic analyses of American consumer culture; and the work of the French scholar Roland Barthes. His book *Mythologies* is another classic work devoted to the semiotics of consumption.

I then dealt with the "looks" of different kinds of stores, with "old towns" as settings for regression and what might be called "innocent" consumption, and with signifiers of luxury on cruise ships. The cruise industry has shown remarkable ingenuity in providing a "luxury" experience, in ships that have many luxurious touches and relatively inexpensive prices.

An understanding of semiotics helps us understand how advertising agencies and everyone involved in selling people things and services achieve their effects. A founding father of semiotics, the American philosopher Charles S. Peirce, said that "the universe is perfused with signs," if it isn't made up exclusively of them. If that's the case, an understanding of how signs work is crucial for making sense of consumer cultures.

Malls . . . vary regarding the extent to which they carry through thematic designs. Yet, they, too, increasingly use overarching motifs and coordinated design schemes in total environments. Malls began . . . in competition not with other malls, . . . but with the downtowns of cities. Their direct competition was for many years the large department stores located in the center of the metropolis. Consequently, they had to advertise themselves as a *place* to go, and they still do. This kind of advertising for a particular space or location within an urban region is . . . aimed at attracting customers to a specific retailing center. As a particular destination, malls require some overarching means of identification. Consequently, as a whole, they often adopt an image meant to be attractive to potential customers who always have the choice of where to do their shopping. In this way they are different from the city downtown, which is not a unified commercial space and does not advertise itself as a location. There are several motifs commonly adopted by malls around the country. One type, called "ye old kitsch," is exemplified by the Olde Towne Mall in Orange County, California. . . . Another frequent motif is called "high tech urban." . . . Malls of this type are several stories high. They have skylighted ceilings that recall the Parisian arcades once studied by Walter Benjamin. They strive for a clean, modern look that accentuates chrome, large plate-glass windows, and flashy neon writing. (1997, 82–83)

—Mark Gottdiener, *The Theming of America:*
Dreams, Visions, and Commercial Spaces

6

MALLS AND THE
AMERICAN CONSUMER CULTURE

There are, it has been estimated, between 1,500 and 2,000 full-scale en-closed malls in the United States, dominated by 300 "fortress" malls—each of which has more than a million square feet and at least three an-chor stores. In his article "An Enormous Landmark Joins Graveyard of Malls," Peter T. Kilborn points out that since 1957, when the first en-closed mall was built, some 300 to 400 malls have been converted to other uses, destroyed, or locked up (*New York Times*, December 24, 2003, p. A10). That's partly because the fortress malls are putting the smaller malls out of business, and it's partly because changing patterns of popula-tion are having an impact. It turns out that when the population around a mall becomes essentially a minority one, whites stop going to the mall and it tends to falter.

DEATH OF A MALL

Kilborn's article deals with the death of the Mall of Memphis, a 160-store mall where only 13 stores are still in business. The building had ninety acres of roof and parking lots, and it went out of business in Christmas of 2003. It was built to mimic a typical rural Main Street; but it looked like a Main Street in a ghost town when Kilborn visited it. It took ten years to build the Mall of Memphis, and the mall made money for twenty-two years. It was killed by competition from more upscale malls and from the arrival of big-box discount stores like Wal-Mart and Target, and by a shift in population around the mall from white people to people of color and working-class people.

The death of the Mall of Memphis was not unusual. As it was dying, indoor malls in cities such as Los Angeles, San Francisco, Chicago, Dallas, and Milwaukee were also dying. These malls can all be described as weak sisters that couldn't compete with nearby, more upscale super-malls in white, middle-class areas and with other kinds of malls that consumers found more pleasing.

"I am a sociologue . . . I mean, *sociologist*," said Fess. "But my particular interest is in contemporary trends in society, and so, quite naturally, I became interested in postmodernism. . . .

"What we find in America, which is why it fascinates us so much, is the *future*. America represents the future and, alas, we fear France will eventually, perhaps soon, become like America. That is why we are so interested in your shopping malls, your hamburger restaurants, your crazy hotels, your pop artists, your films, and your television shows. It is your media, your society of simulations and pseudo-simulations and virtual realities and make believe that fascinates us so much.

"America is the most well-developed postmodern society," Fess went on, gazing into the middle distance, "and all of us who are interested in what the future holds are drawn irresistibly, as a moth is to a flame, to America. And what's more interesting is that Americans don't know, in their invincible ignorance, they have created the quintessential postmodern society. That is why French sociologists and philosophers are so important. We have a history of explaining America to Americans. I and my colleagues, in a sense, are descendants of de Tocqueville. For the twentieth century, though."

Alain Fess, author of *Minotaur: The Beast in the Shopping Mall* [an analysis of the Mall of America], in Arthur Asa Berger, *Postmortem for a Postmodernist* (Walnut Creek, CA: AltaMira Press, 1997.) (Alain Fess is a fictional author.)

Newer venues such as Internet cafés and businesses in small strip malls are taking consumers away from the traditional mall.

The mall industry reached its zenith in 1978, when sales for each square foot of retail space averaged slightly less than $200 a year. By 1992, that figure had dropped to approximately $160 a year per square foot. This drop is the result of changing patterns of shopping by American consumers. It reflects, among other things, the rapid growth of Internet shopping and the development of mini–strip malls, which may have only ten or fifteen stores in them.

THE MALL OF AMERICA

The largest mall in the United States is the Mall of America, which is a gigantic, fully enclosed mall that was built in 1992 for a cost of $650 million. It has 4.2 million square feet of shopping space, which houses more than 500 stores and department store anchors such as Bloomingdale's, Nordstrom, Macy's, and Sears. Approximately half of the space in the Mall of America is used for retailing. To give shoppers the illusion that they are outdoors, the Mall of America is filled with 400 trees, some 30,000 plants, a man-made mountain, and a waterfall that is four stories high. Parking ramps just a few hundred feet from the mall can accommodate 13,000 cars.

This is the 10th anniversary of the great Mall of America—
some 525 stores four stories high on 78 acres in Bloomington
[Minnesota]. For serious shoppers it is Mecca. For critics of
American culture it is madness. Oblivious to its detractors,
hundreds of millions have made pilgrimages to this retail holy
land in Minnesota. I thought I would come to see it before it
dies.

The Mall of America is a dinosaur. The original owners, the
Ghermezian brothers of Edmonton, Canada, are regaining
operating control of the Mall and say they have ideas to revi-
talize the grand old shoppery. For starters, they and their
partners likely will drive down the street from the Mall of
America and erect 5.7 million more square feet of retail on 42
acres to create a "lifestyle center," a phrase the industry uses
to describe the newest creature in shopping-center paleon-
tology. . . .

Mall of America is a grand old place. But the shopping-
center business is in upheaval. "Big-box" stores are the
biggest thing in retailing—Home Depot, Bed Bath & Beyond, Wal-Mart, Target, Best Buy and the like. They've sur-
faced a new species of shopper—people who shop with a
list, go get it, and get out. In a time-pressed world, their
number is growing. . . .

Big malls need browsers to survive, and so developers are
experimenting with a new design format called "lifestyle centers"—generally with open-air pathways, even apartment
complexes, which are somehow supposed to create the long-
lost pedestrian experience of "downtown," itself a mythical
concept to many suburban 18-year-olds.

Daniel Henninger, "Mall of America Still Home for Shop 'til You
Drop," Wonder Land, *Wall Street Journal,* October 3, 2003.

The Mall of America has become a tourist destination, one devoted to
shopping, and it draws more people than Walt Disney World does. Of
course, visitors to the mall don't have to pay for admission. There are now
package tours from various parts of America, from England, and from other
countries for shoppers who wish to do their shopping at the Mall of Amer-

ica. To entertain shoppers between purchases, the mall also has a gigantic indoor amusement park.

What will happen to the Mall of America and to the thousands of indoor and outdoor malls that are experiencing difficulties remains to be seen.

CHANGING SHOPPING PATTERNS AT MALLS

The following statistics come from the International Council of Shopping Centers.

In 1996, 14- to 17-year-olds visited malls 52 times on average for 90 minutes per visit. In 2002, they visited malls 52 times at 84 minutes per visit.

In 1996, seniors 65+ visited malls 50 times on average, at 85 minutes per visit. In 2002, they visited malls 45 times, for 81 minutes per visit.

In 2002, larger malls (800,000+ square feet) kept shoppers an average of 76 minutes per visit. In 2002, smaller malls kept visitors 71 minutes per visit.

The amount of time people spend at malls determines, generally speaking, the amount of money they spend. This isn't always the case; for example, some elderly people get their exercise by walking around malls but do not go there to shop. And some teens go to malls to socialize rather than shop. But generally speaking, when people go to malls to shop, the more time they spend at the malls, the more money they spend—in part because of impulse buying.

According to an article by Andy Serwer in *Fortune* (October 1, 2003), there's been an explosion in the amount of retailing outlets in America. The amount of GLA (gross leasable area) is proliferating at what he calls an "insane" rate, as shown in the following chart:

	1986	*2003*
Population	238 million	286 million
Number of malls	24,500	46,400
Square feet	3.5 billion	5.8 billion
GLA per capita	14.7 square feet	20.3 square feet
Debt on credit card	$3,275	$8,900

Andy Serwer, "The Malling of America," *Fortune*, October 1, 2003.

What these figures represent, Serwer suggests, is an overleveraging and overcapacity problem by businesses and by consumers. It is possible to understand, then, why the mall industry is in so much trouble now, especially because these problems are exacerbated by the economic problems America has faced—in particular, the loss of jobs—in recent years.

LIFESTYLE MALLS AND ENCLOSED MALLS

On December 12, 2003, the *Wall Street Week with Fortune* television show had an interesting segment on a new style of malls—so-called lifestyle malls. What's different about these malls? They include housing and a "signature space" (such as an ice-skating rink) that gives the mall an identity. The new lifestyle malls are designed to facilitate people congregating and spending time—and, of course, money.

According to guest Jeff Gunning—who represented RTKL, a mall-designing company—lifestyle malls are characterized by being open air and street oriented, generally with on-street parking. In the following chart I summarize the main differences between lifestyle malls and conventional enclosed malls.

"Lifestyle" Malls	*Enclosed Malls*
Open air	Enclosed
One level	Multilevel
No anchors	Anchors (department stores)
$84 spent per hour	$58 spent per hour
$270 spent per square foot	$240 spent per square foot

Some experts in retailing argue that the day of the enclosed mall is over, though some larger "fortress" malls are doing very well. Enclosed malls are evolving into shopping and entertainment centers, and lots of these malls now have multiplex film theaters and many different kinds of restaurants.

Kurt Barnard, a retail consultant who was also a guest on the show, offered a historical perspective on why malls are experiencing difficulties:

> You see, we have to really look at what it is that made malls so very popular at one time, which goes back now many, many decades. It made them popular simply because they came about at a time when the average woman was basi-

Many of the surviving enclosed malls have become shopping and entertainment centers, featuring multiplex movie theaters and upscale restaurants.

cally what is generally known as a hausfrau, the woman who took care of the kids and who took care of the fact that the husband needed food when he came home after work. Today it's a different story, thank heavens. Today the woman is in the workforce, she earns money, she doesn't have much time. But her mother used to go to the mall on Saturdays, Sundays for entertainment. It was a break from the routine, which of course was very necessary, and she saw it as a form of entertainment and diversion I would say, and at the same time as a source of new ideas for the home. Today's woman doesn't do that. She doesn't need that.

Barnard's point, that the malls developed when our economy made it possible for one wage earner to support a family, is an important one. Because this is no longer the case in many families, the way people use malls has changed. People generally go to malls with an intent to purchase, rather than for diversion. Getting people who go to malls to buy more than they had planned on purchasing is an important part of mall design nowadays.

MEN IN MALLS

According to Paco Underhill, chief executive of Envirosell, a marketing research and consulting company, men behave differently from women in malls. Underhill suggests that it was in malls that many young men first developed a sense of their identities. For men, especially younger men who know what's "hot," shopping in malls is focused on finding what they are looking for. Rather than wandering around and seeing what is available, these young men have the intent to purchase. And they tend to shop by themselves.

Teenage males and young men spend around $290 a year on casual sportswear. This in contrast to men in general, who spend around $245, according to STS Market Research (quoted in David Carr, "For the Newly Stylish Men, Magazines off the Rack," *New York Times*, February 9, 2004, p. C7).

There are now many sources of fashion information for teenagers and young men, such as MTV, sports, magazines like *Maxim*, films, and television shows. Malls have also evolved to attract more men, with expensive restaurants, movies, and, in some malls, nightclubs. Now, shopping for clothes in a mall, which used to be seen as something only women did, has become legitimized for men.

This process, of convincing men that shopping for clothes and cosmetics is acceptable, has been under way for a long time. According to sociologist Charles Winick, it is tied to the desexualization of American life that has been taking place in recent decades. In his book *Desexualization in American Life*, Winick argues that our popular culture shows women becoming stronger and more masculine and men becoming weaker and more feminine. As Winick writes in the introduction to the Transaction edition of his book (originally published in 1968 as *The New People*):

> *Desexualization in American Life* was written during the late 1960s to call attention to significant changes in American life at that time. The changes were occurring in the social and sex roles, social structure, and popular culture of the period. They appeared to be interrelated, mutually reinforcing, and consistent. The book examines trends in a wide range of activities. It looks at the arts, the uses of leisure, what we eat and drink, how we dress, sex roles, how we rear children, and some aspects of history. The exploration reveals a common thread: American life is undergoing a blurring, a homogenization, a neutering. It is almost as if the color and spirit of individual choice and taste are quietly tip-toeing off the national stage, leaving behind a nation of pallid mannequins. . . . The book explores some of the controversy over male and female roles that was beginning to acquire momentum in the 1960s. It examines the trends in male and female participation in a wide range of activities as well as their representation in the popular arts and more serious ones as well. It also

suggests that the unisex mode and the blurring of male/female roles are com-
plexly related to a corresponding flattening of other significant aspects of
American life. (Winick 1995)

This introduction was written in 1995, nearly thirty years after the publication of *The New People*, and represents Winick's assessment of where things
stood relative to his desexualization hypothesis.

Winick's book offers a hypothesis regarding the behavior of men in malls:
They like malls because they have become feminized to a considerable extent, over the years, and their interest in male toiletries and fashions, and
style in general, is to be understood as a reflection of this process of femi-
nization.

MALLS IN MARVELOUS MARIN COUNTY

I live in a small town called Mill Valley, located in southern Marin
County about five miles north of the Golden Gate Bridge. Marin County
is one of the most affluent counties in the United States; it was made famous by a television show satirizing its "I want it all, now" inhabitants. I
belong to a gym that is five miles north of Mill Valley in a small lifestyle
mall called Larkspur Landing. This mall, which is undergoing hard times,
was purchased several years ago by a mall developer who spent millions
sprucing it up. Just recently, that developer sold Larkspur Landing to another mall developer—who thinks, one must assume, it has possibilities
of being revitalized. The mall is anchored by a huge Bed Bath & Beyond
store, established in a building that was once a large supermarket. Larkspur Landing has several empty stores in it, and I can only wonder what
will happen to it.

Just a mile or two down the road south of Larkspur Landing, in Corte
Madera, there are two flourishing outdoor malls. One is quite large; called
the Village, it has a Macy's and a Nordstrom for anchors. Across the road is
another mall, Town and Country, which is smaller than the Village but
newly prospering. It has many restaurants, a supermarket, and various other
upscale specialty stores, including a large REI store and an expensive gym.
Another five miles or so north of Larkspur Landing is a large enclosed mall,
Northgate, which has a Macy's and a Sears, a multiplex film theater, and
many specialty stores. Although originally built as an outdoor mall, Northgate was turned into an indoor mall. It seems to be prospering.

I have not mentioned a mall in Sausalito, just south of Mill Valley, that is not doing well. North of the Northgate mall, in Petaluma (about thirty miles north of the Golden Gate Bridge), is a large outlet mall that also seems to be struggling. You can see from this discussion that there are lots of malls in southern Marin County—too many for their own good, I would imagine.

These malls in Marin are experiencing difficulties not only because of the rather severe economic downturn in California but also, as I just suggested, because there may be too many malls here. They have to compete with each other, and they have to compete with big-box stores like Home Depot, just a few miles away from the Larkspur Landing mall; with Costco big-box stores near Marin and in San Francisco; and with cities such as San Rafael. According to new reports, Wal-Mart wants to build forty gigantic super-stores in California, selling groceries and other products, but this expansion is being fought in various locales. If these Wal-Mart big-box stores are built, the impact on malls in California could be devastating.

SUMMARY

In this chapter I dealt with the death of a typical mall, in Memphis, as representative of the problems that many malls are facing. Then I discussed the Mall of America, built in 1992, which has the distinction of being the largest mall in the world. It is both a shopping site and an entertainment site, and it attracts more people than Walt Disney World does. The difficulties faced by many smaller malls are connected to changing shopping patterns at malls, to the rapidly expanding numbers of malls, and to the amount of footage available for selling goods in these malls.

Next I contrasted enclosed malls and newer "lifestyle" malls, which are much more successful, generally speaking, than enclosed malls. In lifestyle malls, people spend more money, per hour and per square foot, than they do in enclosed malls. Finally, I discussed the malls in southern Marin County near Mill Valley, where I live. Though Marin is one of the most affluent counties in America, many of its malls are experiencing difficulties—partly because of the economic difficulties in California and partly because there may be too many malls in Marin County—as in the rest of the country.

Now that the American economy seems to be picking up, some of the malls that have been experiencing difficulties may survive. If they do, it will be partly because they are adapting to changing consumption patterns and to changes in American society, in general. One thing that emerges from this analysis of malls is that the retail industry is an extremely competitive one: Malls, as well as the companies that make the products sold there, must continually modify themselves and adapt to changes in American culture and society.

Modernity first appears to everyone as it did to Lévi-Strauss, as disorganized fragments, alienating, wasteful, violent, superficial, unplanned, unstable and inauthentic. On second examination, however, this appearance seems almost a mask, for beneath the disorderly exterior, modern society hides a firm resolve to establish itself on a worldwide base.

Modern values are transcending the old divisions between the Communist East and the Capitalist West and between the "developed" and "third" worlds. The progress of modernity ("modernization") depends on its very sense of instability and inauthenticity. For moderns, reality and authenticity are thought to be elsewhere: in other historical periods and other cultures, in purer, simpler lifestyles. In other words, the concerns of moderns for "naturalness," their nostalgia and their search for authenticity are not merely casual and somewhat decadent, though harmless, attachments to the souvenirs of destroyed cultures and dead epochs. They are also components of the conquering spirit of modernity—the grounds of its unifying consciousness.

The central thesis of this book holds the empirical and ideological expansion of modern society to be intimately linked in diverse ways to modern mass leisure, especially to international tourism and sightseeing. (1976, 2–3)

—Dean MacCannell, *The Tourist: A New Theory of the Leisure Class*

7

TOURISM AND CONSUMER CULTURE

Tourism, we must realize, is the largest industry in the world. It comprises different forms of travel (automobile, bus, train, airplane, ship), different places to go (Europe, Asia, South America, North America, and so on), and different things to do upon arriving at a tourist destination (find housing; shop; dine; visit museums; attend plays, ballets, symphonies, and other cultural events). When you add everything up, and consider the amount of money involved in having fleets of airlines and cruise ships; in having hundreds of thousands of hotels, inns, and restaurants to house and feed tourists; in having places that tourists can go for entertainment as well as cabdrivers to get tourists here and there; and in providing things for tourists to buy, you get a mega-industry of the first degree. (The discussion of tourism that follows draws upon material in my book *Deconstructing Travel*.)

DEFINITIONS OF TOURISM

The word *tourist* comes from the Greek word *tornos*, used in referring to a primitive tool for making a circle. Tourists are people who, literally, make circles of varying sizes: they leave from point A (their homes), travel to one or more other points near or far, and then they return to point A. Tourism, as it is conventionally understood, can be described as a form of travel in which a very specific route is taken, generally by a group of travelers. On a tour one moves from place to place, city to city, or even country to country, and rather quickly. ("If it's Thursday, this must be Spain.") Most tours also involve an element of regimentation. ("Will everyone please get on the bus!") Sooner or later, tourists return to their homes, where they started their travel.

There is, let me point out, no universally accepted definition of tourism; it is defined in different ways by scholars and people in the industry. The World Tourist Organization offers the following definition of tourism:

> It comprises the activities of persons traveling to and staying in places outside their usual environment for not more than one consecutive year for leisure, business and other purposes not related to the exercise of an activity remunerated from within the place visited. (www.world-tourism.org/statistics/tsa_project/TSA_in_depth/chapters/ch3-1.htm; accessed May 25, 2003)

This definition is so broad that it is not very useful. Let me, then, offer some details about tourism that will provide more insights into what tourism is. The term *tourism* has, for many people, negative connotations. This is due to (1) the alleged superficiality of the typical tour, (2) the regimentation of some package tours, and (3) the connection of tourism with consumer culture—a subject I will deal with shortly.

Social scientist Dean MacCannell offers another definition of the term *tourist* in his book *The Tourist: A New Theory of the Leisure Class:*

Tourism is the largest industry in the world.

"Tourist" is used to mean two things in this book. It designates actual tourists: sightseers, mainly middle-class, who are at this moment deployed through the entire world in search of experience. I want the book to serve as a sociological study of this group. But I should make it known that, from the beginning, I intended something more. The tourist is an actual person, or real people are actually tourists. At the same time, "the tourist" is one of the best models for modern-man-in-general. I am equally interested in "the tourist" in this second, metasociological sense of the term. Our first apprehension of modern civilization, it seems to me, emerges in the mind of the tourist. (Mac-Cannell 1976, 1)

For MacCannell, then, tourists are middle-class sightseers searching for experience; they also, it turns out, function as prototypes for modern man. If you push this idea to its logical conclusion, to be a human being—or, more precisely, a modern man or woman—is to be a tourist. *Homo sapiens* has given way to *Homo tornos*. But since tourists are, above all, consumers, you can say that *Homo tornos* is really *Homo consumens*.

ATTRIBUTES OF TOURISM

Many people make a distinction between tourists and travelers. Travelers go places and then come back, often for business; but so do tourists. So, what is a tourist? Tourism, as I interpret the word, has the following attributes:

- It is tied to *leisure* and *pleasure* and *consumer culture.*
- It is done for *pleasure, entertainment,* and related considerations.
- It is *voluntary,* done by choice.
- It is done in *foreign* lands or distant places.
- It is *discretionary,* done because the tourist desires to do so.
- It is *temporary,* for a relatively short period of time.
- It is *not involved with business* and earning money while abroad.
- It is based on a *round trip,* tied to a return to one's point of origin.
- It is made possible by *technological developments* in travel and communication, among other things.
- It is a *mass phenomenon,* done by large numbers of people.

At times it is difficult to distinguish between travel and tourism, and, for practical purposes, I will consider them to be the same thing. A few years ago, I taught a short course at Heinrich Heine University in Düsseldorf. That made me a traveler. But I also spent a couple of hours in Cologne one weekend to see the great cathedral there. Did that make me a tourist? Or a quasi tourist? Often, I suggest, you get a mixture of tourism and travel. Does devoting a short period of time to business somehow make a tourist a business traveler? If a young woman lives in San Diego and drives to Ensenada, Mexico, for lunch, is she a tourist or a traveler?

The difference between travel and tourism has, I would suggest, historical roots. Many years ago, travel was generally something done by elites. Then, when the various means of mass transportation developed—highways, automobiles, railroads, airplanes, cruise ships—travel became available to the average person; this kind of travel is now often described as tourism. That means that defining tourism is based on the ideological belief system of the person, who may label some people as "tourists" and others as "travelers." Tourism is based upon a powerful desire to see the world, to have enriching experiences in other cultures, to go where great events took place, to see beautiful places, to experience what the world can offer us.

CONSUMER COMPULSIONS IN TOURISM

French sociologist Jean Baudrillard suggests there is a latent element of compulsion that can be found in tourism and all forms of consumption. Consumption, Baudrillard explains, must not be seen as a pleasure or a means of enjoyment, but as a duty. Enjoyment and consumption are now the required "business" of the typical consumer, who is now, so it seems, in a situation in which he or she is forced to have fun.

In a passage from Baudrillard's *Consumer Society: Myths and Structures,* which I quoted earlier (see chapter 1), he makes reference to certain kinds of experiences people want. Recall that Baudrillard's analysis involves travel and experiencing the differences found in various cultures. One is obliged to travel to various sites for maximizing gratifications.

TOURISM AS A FORM OF METACONSUMPTION

I describe tourism as a kind of "metaconsumption" because, unlike other forms of consumption, it involves continual expenses. In some cases, as when people book tours that cover everything, these expenses are paid for up front. But in most cases, once a tour is booked, or independent travelers have decided on a place to visit, tourists incur other expenses. Here are some of the most common of these additional expenses:

Collecting souvenirs and sending postcards are some of the "metaconsumption" activities we engage in as tourists.

- Airline tickets or train tickets
- Transportation to and from airport
- Transportation in cities and places being visited
- Hotels
- Meals in restaurants
- Admission to museums, sports events, and cultural events

Having to find good hotels and restaurants, and securing tickets for ball games, operas, or whatever activities they like, can make tourists quite anxious. This may explain, in part, why cruising has become such an important part of the travel and tourism industry.

CRUISING AS A DIFFERENT KIND OF METACONSUMPTION

Cruising is also a form of metaconsumption, but it is different. When purchasing a cruise, tourists pay up front for all their meals and entertainment as well as all kinds of other activities (such as minicourses on massage, fitness workshops, lectures on various subjects, and dance lessons). And they get to visit—admittedly for only short periods of time—the various cities, islands, or other places near the ports where the cruise ships dock.

Passengers eat very fine food (and as much of it as they want) on the ship—in the elegant restaurants and at the buffet lines. Evening meals usually feature five or six courses, beautifully cooked and presented. My wife and I recently took a Caribbean cruise on the Celebrity *Zenith*. There were approximately 1,300 passengers and around 650 crew members. Also on the ship were 120 cooks and pastry chefs—approximately one cook for every ten passengers.

Tourists can, of course, find additional ways to spend money while on a cruise—on drinks, on gambling, on specialty restaurants, and on tours offered by the cruise companies. But they don't have to spend any more than they paid for the cruise and the obligatory tips. Some travel experts suggest that the best deal on cruises is to purchase "inside" staterooms—those without windows—since all the action on cruises takes place in social venues: the theaters, decks, bars, swimming pools, and restaurants. On many cruise ships, as I pointed out earlier, these inside staterooms can cost as little as $50 per person per day, though they tend to average between $70 and $100.

Because of the value-for-money aspects of ocean cruising, the cruise industry has grown enormously in recent decades—by approximately 1,400 percent since 1970. While 500,000 people took cruises in 1970, some 7 million took them in 2000; the industry estimates that by 2010, some 21 million people will take cruises. One reason for this, as I suggested earlier, is that cruising relieves tourists of so many responsibilities, especially the need to continually spend money, which is psychologically draining for many people.

Cruising is essentially a resort experience, and there are, of course, a variety of other resort or travel packages with an up-front payment covering most expenses. Generally, these tours don't cover all of the travelers' meals, but in some cases, one payment includes everything—even drinks. Either way, package deals provide a convenient way for tourists to plan their consumption in advance.

SUMMARY

Because tourism is the largest industry in the world, it makes sense to consider its role in consumer cultures. I suggest that tourism and travel be considered, for all practical purposes, the same thing—even though it is possible to distinguish between business travelers, who go places because they need to do their work, and tourism, which is essentially a leisure activity. The central attribute of tourism—going someplace and then returning to where you started from, making a circle—is common to both business travel and tourism.

There are, as Baudrillard has said, compulsions in our consumer cultures that often relate to tourism. He suggests various activities that people might indulge in and that involve travel in order to be fully realized. Ironically, in our new consumer cultures, we feel "forced" to have fun. It has become an obligation. This leads to my analysis of tourism as a form of what I call "metaconsumption." That is, tourism is a kind of consumption that requires further consumption. Once a destination is decided upon, all kinds of other expenses are engendered.

Finally, I deal with ocean travel and cruising, a form of metaconsumption that has the psychological advantage of requiring most expenses to be paid in one payment, up front. All other purchases on cruises are made with credit cards. This releases tourists from the need to constantly spend money. Due to the economies of scale (in purchasing food, for example) that cruise lines can take advantage of, the cost of cruises is often quite reasonable. For the price of a decent hotel room, two people can enjoy the luxurious kind of travel found on cruise ships—explaining, in part, why cruising has become such a popular way of traveling.

Everything is relative, of course. Only around 15 percent of the American public takes cruises, but 15 percent of 280 million people is a large number: more than 40 million. I recently heard a radio show in which it was asserted that 15 percent of Americans have passports. Even though large numbers of Americans travel to foreign countries, on a per capita basis we lag far behind such countries as England, France, Germany, and Japan. One reason cruising is popular, I would suggest, is that being on these ships provides a sense of security for many people who have anxieties about traveling in foreign countries.

The Smiths
...
They shopped
Till They
Dropped !
1930 — 2004

kept going

All societies have always wasted, ·squandered, expended and consumed beyond what is strictly necessary for the simple reason that it is in the consumption of surplus, of a superfluity that the individual—and society—feel not merely that they exist, but that they are alive. That consumption may go so far as *consummation*, pure and simple destruction, which then takes on a specific social function. In potlatch, for example, it is the competitive destruction of precious goods which sets the seal on social organization. The Kwakiutl sacrifice blankets, canoes, etched "coppers," which they burn or throw into the sea to "maintain their rank," to assert their value. And, again, it is by "wasteful expenditure" that the aristocratic classes have asserted their preeminence down through the ages. (1998, 43)

—Jean Baudrillard, *The Consumer Society: Myths and Structures*

8

BUYER'S REMORSE

The phrase "buyer's remorse" suggests a psychological dimension to consumption. The term *remorse* means a feeling we have that we've done something wrong, that we've made some kind of a mistake. It isn't unusual for people, after they've made a major purchase, to feel a touch of remorse as they wonder whether they've done the right thing, gotten the best deal. One function of advertising is to convince us, before we buy something and after we've made a purchase, that it was an intelligent choice, that we did the right thing.

We are descended, so anthropologists tell us, from hunters and gatherers. This primal urge has been distorted, I would suggest, from a primary focus or emphasis on socially valuable production into privatized consumption. We spend an enormous amount of energy, nowadays, on hunting for bargains and gathering goods for our families and ourselves—with little regard for the social impact of our behavior.

TRAVELING LIGHT

When I was young, in my bohemian days, I wanted to "travel light." By that I meant that I didn't want to be weighed down by all the possessions that most people had—a house and furniture and stereos and all that. But after I got married and had a couple of children, I found myself owning a house full of things—toys, cribs, strollers, bikes, and, later, computers and stereo systems.

How much stuff do we need? A consumer culture brings with it a number of social implications.

Recently, I took an inventory of the things in my house and was astonished to find that in addition to the furniture one needs to live—a bed, dressers, tables, and chairs—I had four television sets (none larger than thirteen inches), two computers (I'd given away three old ones), six radios, ten bookcases (and thousands of books), a microwave, a blender, a Cuisinart, an electric espresso maker, an electric knife, a viola, a piano, two cars, two bikes, and so on.

Relatively speaking, I'm still traveling light. Our neighbors, who have three daughters, have six cars parked in their driveway. God only knows how many cell phones, stereos, and iPods they might own. Over the years, and as new kinds of gizmos and gadgets become "indispensable," people collect more and more things. The question is, how much do you need? How many pants and suits or skirts and dresses does a person need? Where do you draw the line between having enough stuff to enjoy a good life and having too much stuff?

THE PROBLEM IS DISTRIBUTION

America is the wealthiest nation in the world; yet, we have large numbers of people living in poverty and millions of people with no health care insurance. The problem is in distribution. As I pointed out earlier, the distribution of wealth in the United States is tilted toward an upper 1 percent of the population that owns most of the wealth.

The children of the wealthy have better "life chances" than do the children of middle-class and poor people. Children of privilege have access to excellent medical care, to the best primary school and secondary school education, and to the better colleges and universities. The playing field is not level in America, not by any means.

The problem we face is structural. People want all kinds of goods and services, but they don't want to pay taxes for them. Recently I heard a University of California professor, George Lakoff, discuss this matter. He said we should think of taxes as being like dues that we pay to belong to an organization. We pay dues and we get certain benefits. Relatively speaking, Americans pay much less in taxes than people in other countries do; and the richest Americans—and American corporations, in my opinion as well as that of many others—pay much less than they should.

In America, the middle classes are being squeezed. Many people are falling out of the middle classes due to inequities in our tax system and the difficulties the American economy is now undergoing. If we taxed our corporations and those at the top properly, and made them pay their fair share, I believe that we would have enough tax revenue to pay for services that people want—and, in many cases, need. We are, after all, the only industrial country in the Western world that does not provide health insurance for everyone in the country.

OVERWORKED AMERICANS

In order to survive, Americans work too hard and too long. While most workers in European countries get four to six weeks of vacation, the typical American worker gets two weeks of vacation and sometimes—after several years of service—three weeks. That isn't enough for people to travel, to rest, to recharge their batteries. Psychologists have found that it is important for people to go on vacations and get away from their everyday routines for a while. But many Americans are not able to do this.

It seems that because of their desire for material goods, and in some cases out of economic necessity, Americans work more hours nowadays and take fewer vacations. Some Americans take no vacations, and others work many more hours of overtime than is good for them.

Thus, consumption may reflect a means of assuaging a hidden rage in people, who do not recognize that they are using their buying power as a means of dealing with the psychological anxieties and anger they feel. For people who see themselves as caught on some kind of a treadmill, buying

things represents one of the few gratifications they can obtain. We consume
the way we do because we've been taught to act that way.

HEROES OF PRODUCTION AND HEROES
OF CONSUMPTION

Sociologist Leo Lowenthal made a study of biographies in popular magazines during 1901–1914 and 1940–1941 and found that interesting changes
had taken place. As he writes in "Biographies in Popular Magazines" (1944):

> If a student in some very distant future should use popular magazines of
> 1941 as a source of information as to what figures the American public
> looked to in the first stages of the greatest crisis since the birth of the
> Union, he would come to a grotesque result. While the industrial and pro-
> fessional endeavors are geared to a maximum of speed and efficiency, the
> idols of the masses are not, as they were in the past, the leading names in
> the battle of production, but the headliners of the movies, the ball parks
> and the night clubs. While we found that around 1900 and even around
> 1920 the vocational distribution of magazine heroes was a rather accurate
> reflection of the nation's living trends, we observe that today the hero-
> selection corresponds to needs quite different from those of genuine infor-
> mation. They seem to lead to a dream world of the masses who no longer
> are capable or willing to conceive of biographies primarily as a means of ori-
> entation and education. They receive information not about the agents and
> methods of social production but about the agents and methods of social
> and individual consumption.

*Do fans idolize the rich and famous for what they produce or what
they consume?*

These magazines changed from featuring what Lowenthal called "heroes of production" to "heroes of consumption," and it can be argued that since the 1940s, in the popular press, the focus is not on what our heroes and heroines create but what they consume. Since people tend to identify with and imitate their heroes and heroines, they are led, then, to focus their attention on shopping and consuming goods and services. Our heroes, Lowenthal points out, not only entertain us, but they also educate us—in ways that are not always valuable or in our self-interest.

YOU ARE WHAT YOU DRIVE

A recent commercial for Toyota automobiles featured the slogan "You are what you drive." What this slogan suggests is that our identities are tied up with our automobiles, which we use as signifiers of our being successful and able to afford certain kinds or brands of cars. Someone I know once told me, with a sense of pride, "We're a two-Lexus family." He had noticed my 1984 Toyota Corolla and my wife's 1990 Camry on our car deck.

For many people, being able to purchase an expensive car is of great importance to their sense of themselves, for it indicates a certain amount of financial (and, connected to this, sexual) power. To my mind this is a rather pathetic situation, probably connected to an unrecognized sense of inferiority. But as long as the automobile companies are able to persuade people that "you are what you drive," and that this is important because people notice and judge you by what you drive, people will be captives to these companies and their insidious sales pitches.

NEEDS ARE FINITE, DESIRES ARE INFINITE

In the final analysis, it boils down to this: Needs are finite but desires are infinite. We don't need all the stuff we buy; but we feel that having things will make our lives better, make us feel more "alive," as Baudrillard points out in the quotation that opens this chapter. This explains, in part, why there is so much energy and innovation in capitalist societies. There is, in people, a voracious hunger not only to explore the world, but to possess it—or as much of it as is possible. Thus millionaires and billionaires, who need not work, continually seek to expand their empires and make even more money.

One solution to the problem of the skewed distribution of income in America is to find ways to rectify the situation by paying workers more and

In postmodern societies, consumers emphasize their "lifestyles" and continually buy new products—such as cars, clothes, music CDs, and other accessories—to maintain them.

taxing wealthy corporations more. This will make it possible for those who consume less than they should to consume, at the very least, as much as they need—both in goods and in services. That is, we need to find ways to equalize consumption and spread it out more evenly. We need a certain amount of goods in order to feel that our lives are meaningful. How much is, of course, relative to where we live and what those around us have and don't have. As it now stands in America, a relatively small percentage of the population has almost infinite consumption power, while large numbers of people live in relative poverty.

POSTMODERN SOCIETIES ARE CONSUMPTION SOCIETIES

We are now living, so philosophers and other savants tell us, in postmodern societies—characterized by widespread doubts about the large, overarching philosophical systems that formerly justified things to people. One important attribute of postmodern societies is that they are consumer societies. In postmodern societies, people make their "lifestyles" a central organizing factor or project in their lives. To maintain these lifestyles, which continually change, they have to keep purchasing clothes and other objects.

Thus, except for a small percentage of people who opt out of our consumer societies for ethical or other reasons, most people are caught up in the frenzy of consumption in order to maintain a given lifestyle or change to another one that seems preferable. Each of us becomes our own life project, as we attempt to turn our lives into some kind of approximation of a work of art—wearing the trendiest fashions, eating in the best restaurants, living in houses full of designer objects that reflect our aesthetic sensibilities. Caught up in this process, we tend to neglect our social obligations and forget about the debt we owe to society and its institutions—educational and otherwise—that have made our lifestyles possible.

The problem is that, in many cases, we become so wrapped up in our new and continually changing lifestyles that we lose our identities—any sense of who we really are. But, postmodernists would argue, who cares? A coherent identity, a sense of "self," postmodernists would suggest, is a modernist notion—and modernism petered out in the 1960s. So, for the moment, the game goes on. And where it will all lead—aside from huge dumps filled with the mountains of junk we throw away—is anyone's guess.

REFERENCES

Barthes, Roland. 1972. *Mythologies*. New York: Hill & Wang.

Baudrillard, Jean. 1998. *The consumer society: Myths and structures*. Thousand Oaks, CA: Sage.

Berger, Arthur Asa. 2004. *Ads, fads, and consumer culture*. Lanham, MD: Rowman & Littlefield.

———. 2004. *Deconstructing travel: Cultural and anthropological perspectives on the tourist experience*. Walnut Creek, CA: AltaMira Press.

Bowlby, Rachel. 1997. Supermarket futures. In Falk and Campbell, *The shopping experience*.

Cohen, Adam. 2002. *The perfect store: Inside eBay*. Boston: Little, Brown.

Danesi, Marcel. 2002. *Understanding media semiotics*. London: Arnold.

Dichter, Ernest. 2002. *The strategy of desire*. New Brunswick, NJ: Transaction.

Douglas, Mary. 1997. In defence of shopping. In Falk and Campbell, *The shopping experience*.

Eliade, Mircea. 1961. *The sacred and the profane: The nature of religion*. New York: Harper Torchbooks.

Falk, Pasi, and Colin Campbell, eds. 1997. *The shopping experience*. London: Sage.

Featherstone, Mike. 1991. *Consumer culture and postmodernism*. Thousand Oaks, CA: Sage.

Frith, Katherine T., ed. 1997. *Undressing the ad: Reading culture in advertising*. New York: Peter Lang.

Girard, René. 1991. *A theater of envy: William Shakespeare*. New York: Oxford University Press.

Gottdiener, Mark. 1997. *The theming of America: Dreams, visions, and commercial spaces.* Boulder, CO: Westview.

Greenwald, Rachel. *Find a husband after 35 using what I learned at Harvard Business School.* New York: Ballantine, 2003.

Haug, Wolfgang F. 1971. *Critique of commodity aesthetics: Appearance, sexuality, and advertising in capitalist society.* Trans. Robert Bock. Minneapolis: University of Minnesota Press.

Le Bon, Gustave. 1960. *The crowd: A study of the popular mind.* New York: Viking Press.

Lowenthal, Leo. 1944. Biographies in popular magazines. In Lazarsfeld and Stanton, eds., *Radio Research 1942–1943.*

Lyotard, Jean-François. 1984. *The postmodern condition: A report on knowledge.* Trans. Geoff Bennington and Brian Massumi. Minneapolis: University of Minnesota Press.

MacCannell, Dean. 1976. *The tourist: A new theory of the leisure class.* New York: Schocken Books.

McLuhan, Marshall. 1951. *The mechanical bride: Folklore of industrial man.* Boston: Beacon Press.

Pappenheim, Fritz. 1967. *The alienation of modern man.* New York: Monthly Review Press.

Patai, Raphael. 1972. *Myth and modern man.* Englewood Cliffs, NJ: Prentice-Hall.

Riviere, Joan. 1964. Hate, greed, and aggression. In Klein and Riviere, *Love, Hate, and Reparation.* New York: W. W. Norton & Company.

Saussure, Ferdinand de. 1966. *A course in general linguistics.* New York: McGraw-Hill.

Schwartz, Barry. 2004. When it's all too much. *Parade,* January 4.

Solomon, Michael, Gary Bamossy, and Soren Askegaard. 2002. *Consumer behavior: A European perspective.* 2nd ed. Harlow, England: Financial Time Prentice-Hall.

Thompson, Michael, Richard Ellis, and Aaron Wildavsky. 1990. *Cultural theory.* Boulder, CO: Westview Press.

Van Tassel, David D., and Robert W. McAharen, eds. 1969. *European origins of American thought.* Chicago: Rand McNally.

Weber, Max. 1958. *The Protestant ethic and the spirit of capitalism.* New York: Scribners.

Weiss, Michael. 1988. *The clustering of America.* New York: Harper & Row.

Wernick, Andrew. 1991. *Promotional culture: Advertising, ideology and symbolic expression.* Thousand Oaks, CA: Sage.

Winick, Charles. 1995. *Desexualization in American life.* Classics in Communication and Mass Culture. New Brunswick, NJ: Transaction.

Zollo, Peter. 1999. *Wise up to teens: Insights into marketing and advertising to teenagers.* 2nd ed. Ithaca, NY: New Strategist Publications.

Zukin, Sharon. *How shopping changed American culture.* New York: Routledge, 2003.

INDEX

Ads, Fads, and Consumer Culture, x, 25–28

Alienation of Modern Man, 79–80

Amazon.com, x, 61, 62

American Idol, 54

American Idol turned into a brand, 40

Askegaard, Soren, 36, 68

Bamossy, Gary, 36, 68

Barnard, Kurt, 104–5

Barthes, Roland, 88, 91–92, 96

Baudrillard, Jean, 16–17, 20, 114, 118

Baxter, Richard, 7–8

"Biographies in Popular Magazines," 122

Bowlby, Rachel, 57

Burne, Jerome, 76–77

Buyer's remorse, 119–25

Calendar and shopping: back to school, 64–65; Christmas, 66–67; Halloween, 65–66; Super Bowl, 63–64; Thanksgiving, 66

Calvin, John, 5–7, 17–18

Carr, David, 106

Claritas 66

Clustering of America, 30–31

clusters of consumers, 31–32; PRIZM typology, 28–32

Coca-Cola, 76–77

Cohen, Adam, 62

Cohen, Marshall, 37

Consumer Behavior: A European Perspective, 36, 68

consumer culture: American Dream and, 23; automobiles and identity, 123; calendar, 63–67; children as consumers, 32–34; consuming as an activity, 3; defined, x, 1–2; development in America, 7; distribution of wealth in America, 21–25; Grid-Group typology and, 8–13; heroes of production and heroes of consumption, 122–23; higher-income delusion, 22–25; impact of Calvinist thought on, 5–6; malls and, 99–109; nationalities and, 40–42;

needs are finite, desire are infinite, 123–24; other kinds of cultures, 14–15; overworked Americans, 121–22; postmodernism and, 16–18; postmodern societies and, 124–25; problem of distribution of wealth, 120–21; production culture, x; psychographics and consumption, 25–28; realms of choice and actions, 15; relation to Protestant Ethic, 6–7; sacred roots of, 4–8; teenagers as consumers, 36–40; traveling light, 119–20; tweens as consumers, 34–36

Consumer Culture and Postmodernism, 2

Consumer Reports, 47

Consumer Society: Myths and Structures, 16–17, 118

consumption: as dramatic narrative, 51–52; Big-Box stores, 58–59; chain of, 52–53; department stores, 56; give ourselves rewards, 48–49; importance of sales, 47-48 linguistic obfuscation and self-delusion, 59–60; means of showing creativity, 49–50; means toward being perceived, 46–47; mimetic desire and, 54–55; modes of, 60–63; myth and, 70–73; psychological aspects of, 45–50; psychology of, 73–81; status symbols as signs of success, 50–51; supermarkets and super drugstores, 57

Costco, 58, 61

Course in General Linguistics, x

Cringely, Robert X., 61

Critique of Commodity Aesthetics: Appearance, Sexuality, and Advertising in Capitalist Society, 51, 55

The Crowd, 83, 87

Cultural Theory, 8–11

Danesi, Marcel, 88

Death of a Salesman, 80

Deconstructing Travel, xiii

demographics: catchy names and, 28; Claritas corporation, 28–32; PRIZM typology and, 28–30

"Department Stores Launch Counter-Attack," 52

Desexualization in American Life (The New People), 106–7

Dichter, Ernest, 44–46, 48–50, 67, 73

Douglas, Mary, 8–9, 11–13, 18, 28, 81, 82

Dubrow, Joel S., 76

eBay, 61–63

Economist magazine, 40–41, 42

Edwards, Jonathan, 15

Eliade, Mircea, 70–73

Ellis, Richard, 8, 11, 12

Emerson, Ralph Waldo, 18

Envirosell, 105

European Origins of American Thought, 5

Featherstone, Mike, 2, 4

Financial Times, 52, 77

Find a Husband After 35, 80–81

"For the Newly Stylish Men, Magazines Off the Rack," 106

Fortune magazine, 103

Foster, Lauren, 52

Freud, Sigmund, 46, 75–76, 86

Girard, René, 54

Google, x

Gottdiener, Mark, 98

Greenwald, Rachel, 80, 86

Grid-Group typology: egalitarians, 9–10; elitists, 9–10; explained, 8; fatalists, 9–10; four consumer cultures, 8–13; individualists, 9–10;

power of cultural alignments, 12;
    problem of freedom, 12–13
Gunning, Jeff, 104

Hanson, Graeme, 78
"Hate, Greed and Aggression," 44
Haug, Wolfgang, 51, 55
Henninger, Daniel, 102
Home Depot, 61
Horvitz, Bruce, 63

"If the Pros Use a Tool or a
    Toothbrush, It Will Sell," 85
"In Defense of Shopping," 11–13

Keveney, Bill, 40
Key to the Consumer, 51–52
Kilborn, Peter T., 99

Lakoff, George, 121
Le Bon, Gustav, 83, 86
Lehrer News Hour, 74
Levin, Diane, 34
Linn, Susan, 34
Lowenthal, Leo, 122–23
Lyotard, Jean-François, 16

MacCannell, Dean, 110, 112–13
"Mall of America Still Home for Shop
    'til You Drop," 102
Malls and American consumer culture,
    99–109
changing shopping patterns at malls,
    103–4
death of the Mall of Memphis, 99–100
lifestyle malls and enclosed malls,
    104–5
male behavior in malls, 105–7
Mall of America, 101–3
malls in Marin county, 107–8
Marcus, Stanley, 56
Marx, Karl, 10, 11, 16

McAharen, Robert W., 5, 6
McLuhan, Marshall, 90–91, 96
Mechanical Bride: The Folklore of
    Industrial Man, 90–91, 96
Miller, Arthur, 80
myth: camouflaged in contemporary
    culture, 70–71; definitions of,
    70–71; importance of houses,
    72–73; of nature and American
    culture, 71–72
Myth and Modern Man, 71
Mythologies, 91–92, 96

Nasser, Haya El, 33
Newsweek magazine, 82
New York Times, 32, 37, 106

Omo, 92
Overberg, Paul, 33

Pappenheim, Fritz, 79–80
Paradox of Choice, 73–75
Patai, Raphael, 71
Pavlov, Ivan, 76
Pay-Pal, 62
Peirce, Charles S., 97
Pepsi Cola, 77
Perfect Store: Inside eBay, 62
Persil, 92
Point of Purchase: How Shopping
    Changes American Culture, 84
Postmodern Condition: A Report on
    Knowledge, 16
postmodernism: compulsion to
    consume, 16–17; consumer cultures
    and, 16–18; definition, 16;
    "incredulity toward metanarratives,"
    16; modernism and, 16–17
Postmortem for a Postmodernist, 100
Promotional Culture: Advertising,
    Ideology and Symbolic
    Expression, 20

Protestant Ethic and the Spirit of Capitalism, 6–7
psychographics: marketing typologies chart, 26; VALS (Values and Lifestyles typologies), 25–27
psychology of consumption: collectors, 77–79; id, ego, and superego relationships and, 75; marketing personality, 79, 80; maximizers and satisfizers, 73–75; neuromarketing, 76–77; Pavlovian perspective on, 76

Riviere, Joan, 44
Rozhon, Tracie, 37

Sacred and Profane, 70
San Francisco Chronicle, 33, 34, 78
Saussure, Ferdinand de, x, 12, 14, 18, 27
Schwartz, Barry, 73–74, 86
Sears, 61, 62
semiotics: defined, 89; old towns, 94–95; Roland Barthes and, 88; shopping and, 89–97; signifiers of luxury on cruises, 95–96; stores as settings for consumption, 92–94
Serwer, Andy, 103–4
Seth, Suhel, 40–41
Shanghai Tatler magazine, 42
ship 'n shore cruise connoisseurs, 96
Shopping Experience, 57
Smith, Leslie, 85
sociology of consumption: crowds and consumer behavior, 83–84; fads and crazes, 82–83; four consumer cultures or lifestyles, 82; upscale, downscale, entry-level, top of the line, 84–85; you are where you shop, 84
Solomon, Michael, 36, 68
Strategy of Desire, 44–46, 48–50

Target, 56
Tassel, David Van, 5, 6
teenagers: advertising and preferences, 38; consumption and, 36–40; coolest brands, 38; "The eBay Way: How Auction Sites Like eBay Turn Retail Economics on Its Ear for the Betterment of Just about Everybody," 61–62; high school cliques, 29; segmentation system for, 37–38; TRU (Teen Research Unlimited), 37; *Theming of America: Dreams, Visions, and Commercial Spaces,* 98
Thompson, Michael, 8, 9–13
tourism: as form of metaconsumption, 114–15; attributes of, 113–14; consumer compulsions and, 114; cruising and, 115–16; defined, 111–13; largest industry in world, 111
Tourist: A New Theory of the Leisure Class, 110, 112
TRU (Teen Research Unlimited), 37–40

Underhill, Paco, 105–6
Understanding Media Semiotics, 88
USA Today, 33, 37, 40, 63, 85

Victoria's Secret, 61

Wall Street Journal, 55, 76, 102
Wall Street Week with Fortune, 104
Wal-Mart, 56, 58, 59, 61, 62
Walt Disney World, 102
Weaver, Greg, 37
Weber, Max, 6–7, 14, 18
Weiss, Michael, 30, 31
Wernick, Andrew, 20
"When Wal-Mart Comes to Town," 58

Wildavsky, Aaron, 8, 11
Winick, Charles, 106–7
Winn, Steven, 78
Wise Up to Teens, 37–38
World Tourist Organization, 112

Zenith cruise ship, 96
Zola, Emile, 57
Zollo, Peter, 37–38
Zukerman, Gregory, 55
Zukin, Sharon, 84

ABOUT THE AUTHOR

Arthur Asa Berger is professor emeritus of broadcast and electronic communication arts at San Francisco State University, where he taught between 1965 and 2003. He graduated in 1954 from the University of Massachusetts, majoring in literature and philosophy. In 1956 he received an M.A. degree in journalism and creative writing from the University of Iowa. He was drafted shortly after graduating from Iowa and served in the U.S. Army in the Military District of Washington in Washington, D.C., where he was a feature writer and speechwriter in the district's Public Information Office. He also covered high school sports for the *Washington Post* on weekend evenings.

Berger spent a year touring Europe after he got out of the army and then went to the University of Minnesota, where he received a Ph.D. in American Studies in 1965. He wrote his dissertation on the comic strip *Li'l Abner*. In 1963–1964, he was awarded a Fulbright Foreign Scholarship to Italy and taught at the University of Milan. In 1984 he spent a year as visiting professor at the Annenberg School for Communication at the University of Southern California, in Los Angeles.

Berger is the author of numerous articles, book reviews, and more than fifty books on the mass media, popular culture, humor, and everyday life. Among his recent books are *Ads, Fads, and Consumer Culture; Media and Society; Making Sense of Media: Key Texts in Media and Cultural Studies; Ocean Travel and Cruising; Deconstructing Tourism; The Art of Comedy Writing;* and *Video Games: A Popular Culture Phenomenon.* He has also written several comic academic mysteries, including *Postmortem for a Postmodernist; The Mass Comm Murders: Five Media Theorists Self-Destruct;* and *Durkheim Is Dead: Sherlock Holmes Is Introduced to Sociological Theory.* Berger's books have been translated into Italian, German, Swedish, Chinese, Korean, Indonesian, and Russian, and he has lectured in more than a dozen countries in the course of his career.

Berger is married, has two children and two grandchildren, and lives in Mill Valley, California. He enjoys travel and dining in ethnic restaurants. He can be reached by e-mail at aberger@sfsu.edu or arthurasaberger@yahoo.com.